The Original Eye

Ceux pour lesquels le monde visible existe
Théophile Gautier

The Original Eye

Arbiters of Twentieth-Century Taste

Philip Core

Prentice-Hall, Inc., Englewood Cliffs, N.J. 07632

Library of Congress Cataloging in Publication Data

Core, Philip.
   The original eye: arbiters of twentieth-century taste.

   Includes index.
      1. Avant-garde (Aesthetics)—History—20th century.
2. Arts, Modern—20th century.   3. Art patrons—Biography.
4. Artists—Biography.   5. Popular culture.   I. Title.
NX456.C68   1984   700'.92'2   83-22924
ISBN 0-13-642455-5

FOR C.R.

I am a rose and when I sing
I am a rose like anything
Gertrude Stein

© 1984 by Philip Core
This book was designed and produced by John Calmann and Cooper Ltd.,
71 Great Russell St., London WC1B 3BN, England.

10 9 8 7 6 5 4 3 2 1

ISBN 0-13-642455-4

This book is available at a special discount when ordered in
bulk quantities. Contact Prentice-Hall, Inc., General
Publishing Division, Special Sales, Englewood Cliffs, N.J. 07632

Prentice-Hall International, Inc., *London*
Prentice-Hall of Australia Pty. Limited, *Sydney*
Prentice-Hall Canada Inc., *Toronto*
Prentice-Hall of India Private Limited, *New Delhi*
Prentice-Hall of Japan, Inc., *Tokyo*
Prentice-Hall of Southeast Asia Pte. Ltd., *Singapore*
Whitehall Books Limited, *Wellington, New Zealand*
Editora Prentice-Hall do Brasil Ltda., *Rio de Janeiro*

Contents

1 Jean Cocteau, *enfant terrible* of aesthetic Paris, linked himself to Diaghilev and his troupe in search of the fashionable and the new. Diaghilev's reaction was quizzical, though he commissioned the libretto of *Le Dieu Bleu* from the poet

Introduction

'Astonish me!!!' Sergei Diaghilev

In 1910 Jean Cocteau elected himself a mascot of Diaghilev's *Ballets Russes*. A poet by reputation, Cocteau was eager to design décors, write scenarios, know the leading dancers. A youth of many talents, Cocteau at twenty-one had not yet found his personal style. In fact the Parisian art world saw him as a slightly ridiculous figure, who imitated mannerisms from anyone both brilliant and famous. Nevertheless, the potent charm which served Cocteau all his life worked to a certain extent on Diaghilev, who reluctantly suggested that the young poet write the book for a ballet to music by the French drawing-room composer Reynaldo Hahn. *Le Dieu Bleu* resulted. This overwrought pastiche of the orientalist genre which Diaghilev's *Schéhérazade* and *Cléopâtre* had already made popular was disappointing, leaving little mark on the history of ballet, except for the sumptuous costumes by Léon Bakst which it occasioned. Diaghilev himself took from this damp squib the message that the vogue for exoticism was passing, and turned his ruthless attention to the more avant-garde.

On the night in 1912 when the curtain fell to polite applause on *Le Dieu Bleu* Cocteau, Diaghilev and Nijinsky (who had danced the role of the Blue God) went walking through Paris to unwind after the efforts of the performance. Cocteau, mesmerized by the leader of such a revolution in taste, was in the habit of clowning about the great man. He sought to delight with youthful gaiety a man by whom he wanted to be accepted as a creative personality. Secure in his frivolity, Cocteau was in for a sharp lesson on the nature of the poet's calling. Suddenly, he later recalled, while Nijinsky walked on ahead, bored and sulky, Diaghilev 'made fun of some ridiculous antic of mine. When I asked *why* (I was accustomed to be praised), he stopped, adjusted his monocle, and said: *"Etonne-moi. Astonish me."* '

Astonish me. What was Diaghilev demanding, and why have we used his phrase as a preface to this book? He was asking for that *frisson* André Breton called 'a fresh breeze on the temples' – an electric shock which resulted from contact with real novelty and beauty in any form. Up to 1912 Cocteau had created polite poetry and minor drawings for a society audience. Diaghilev sensed the boy's real genius, gave him a chance to create something new, and made no bones about the fact that he had failed to do so. His words (which Cocteau claimed changed his life) head this book because they perfectly define the role of the personalities it concerns. Diaghilev was an artist who created out of the energy generated by painters, sculptors, designers, choreographers and writers. His talent lay in making them feel they had at all costs to astonish *him*, and that, if they did so, they were guaranteed to have created something which the world could not ignore. So, with those two words, the Russian impresario takes his place with the select few who have fashioned the visual world simply by ensuring that, after them, it would be different. These are the creators of taste for whom the poet Théophile Gautier emphasized, 'the visual world exists'.

Taste, like religion, has its apostles and messiahs. Such personalities create the links in the history of seeing, displaying and being: the linked chain of style. Its messiahs have earned for themselves the title bestowed some fifteen hundred years ago on Petronius, friend of the Emperor Nero. The author of the *Satyricon* was regarded by his peers as the ultimate judge of

niceties in social life and the arts. To him they came with questions of etiquette, dress, entertainment, design. His follies were law to those who desired rules in matters of taste. He was called Petronius Arbiter Elegantiarum – Decider of Elegance – a title since accorded most of the people who were absorbed in an effort to stamp their personalities on all the details of life. Such an attention to detail is the essence of style, and an arbiter can be defined as a person in a socially prominent position who sets a style so definite that it becomes part of history. In the person of Akenaten, the monotheistic pharaoh-poet, Eighteenth-Dynasty Egypt saw the incarnation of a new, naturalistic style in art, worship and monarchy. Pericles of Athens presided over not only a great humanist state, but the unparalleled flowering of all the arts in the golden age of fifth-century Greece. Duke Charles of Burgundy was the peerless knight of late-medieval culture, whose personal taste conjured a whole realm of art, architecture and music around his romantic court. Lorenzo de' Medici, banker prince of fifteenth-century Florence, nurtured such talents as Michelangelo's and Botticelli's in painting and sculpture, Pico della Mirandola's and Machiavelli's in literature, Poliziano's and Fra Paciolo's in philosophy and science, creating the Renaissance itself in his palace. Since that time such egregious figures as Louis XIV (who fused art, politics and society in Versailles, the paradigm of courtly life), Abel Poisson (Marquis de Marigny, Louis XV's Minister of Building, who, together with his sister, Madame de Pompadour, invented the Rococo), Lord Burlington (the English amateur of architecture whose London house now holds the Royal Academy, the Palladio of eighteenth-century neo-classicism) or Napoleon III's Empress, Eugénie (whose nostalgia for the era of Marie-Antoinette infused gaiety and

2 (*Above left*) Robert de Montesquiou, drypoint by Helleu. The caustic 'Professor of Beauty' to *fin-de-siècle* Paris successively championed aesthetic, *art nouveau* and *belle époque* styles for an aristocratic society

3 (*Above right*) The soberly dressed Alfred Stieglitz brought calvinist business acumen to the world of art, founding the durable American market for the avant-garde in his successive galleries

4 Vain and uninhibitedly
American, Elsie Mendl
pursued youthfulness into
extreme old age; her beach
gymnastics were famous

5 Muse of the Surrealists, great original, affluent patroness,
Vicomtesse Marie-Laure de Noailles combined mink and ruins
for Beaton's camera with the somnambulistic elegance of
Cocteau's milieu

6 (*Above left*) Spiritually a couturier, Cecil Beaton brought to his role as arbiter of fashion an eye for female elegance and the nostalgia for past styles which culminated in his great designs for *My Fair Lady*

7 (*Above right*) Filippo Marinetti (centre) with Luca Giordano (right). Closing the gaps between Futurism, Symbolism and Fascism, Marinetti joined the Italian Academy under Mussolini, moved from Florence to Rome, and supported the reign of bullets

luxury into the parvenu Third Empire in France) – have personified the unique but popular obsessions in dress, collecting, entertaining and décor which we lump together under the heading of 'Fashion'.

Fashion is the union of two opposites, which together form a compulsion: on the one hand, to be different, on the other, to subscribe to a common mean. We are all constantly subject to these two urges. In the arbiters of style we find the 'obscure object of desire' demanded by this compulsion. They appear to be both something excitingly *other* than we are, and the personification of a new norm. With the capacity to suggest these qualities comes immortality: not the immortality of a dictator or conqueror, or even a statesman or diplomat, but rather the unforgettable impression of a comet or a beautiful day or a previously untasted food. Just as its artefacts help recreate a culture, so no documents or laws can recall the spirit of a past time as well as do the biographies of these distinguished figures.

Nineteenth-century Romanticism recognized this. The Romantics – painters, poets and personalities – all sought prominence as great originals in taste, morals and aesthetics. They postured to an audience eager for new poses, who quickly adopted even the most extreme manifestations of this cult of individuality. This success created a self-perpetuating demand that each style have its unique impresario. The result was to litter the century with revolts, cabals, manifestos, cliques, cults – each under the inspiration of a particular 'star' (this word itself came from the Romantic Ballet's *danseuse étoile* or lead ballerina, some of whom, like Marie Taglioni and Fanny Elssler, set styles in dress and coiffure which place them among

8 In some ways Peggy Guggenheim remained a typical American rich girl: her pack of noisy dogs was a cliché for spoilt ladies of the era. Her entourage of artists sometimes felt themselves in the same position

the minor arbiters of taste). By 1900 snobbery had replaced even religion as a moral power, creating idols of elegance (chosen from the aristocracy) or of modernism (chosen from the artists) to lay down what was or was not done by those who mattered.

Life today is no different, is, in fact, derived in many ways from the brash and egocentric religion of individuality which balanced Victorian prudery. With its passion for speed, our century has merely cut down the 'shelf-life' of novelties in lifestyle, while simultaneously multiplying by millions the audience for such novelties. The effect of this has been to cancel the well-mannered evolution of history's aesthetic cycles. This is the principle of revolutionary reaction, the thrill of the avant-garde, an appropriately explosive kick for our neurotic century. The very nature of style in this century consists in an explosive quality. The revolutions of politics and wars have left their mark, and social life now demands an imperious banishment of the obsolete to make place for the unprecedented. For economic reasons this aesthetic of novelty stimulates industrial production. In advertising we have come to accept the stereotypes which have resulted from the marriage of industry and style. The emergence of photography floodlit the idols of the market-place, making the original an immediately accessible reality in newspapers, magazines and, eventually, films. The arbiters had never been so visible, and they adapted themselves to this brighter limelight. From the decadent nostalgia of 1900 to the mass nostalgia of our new decade, this has been the first century of taste to be completely reported by the camera. This book sets out to illustrate the epochs of the camera century, not by dates, but by style's ebb and flow.

Photography has stared more fixedly at our heroes of state than painting ever did. In a tiny snapshot we can see people larger than life. We have become adept at the long-dreamt-of magic of Fashion: to make time stand still, to immortalize change itself. To the figures we see

9 (*Above left*) In the received tradition of commercial art, Andy Warhol will turn his hand and image to (apparently) any profit-making cause. Here, with a new face, a new wig and a new series of ecological silkscreens, he enters the Eighties with a resurrected trendiness

10 (*Above right*) The clean, easily recognizable quality of ugly Punk (gorgeous as Carpaccio costume in retrospect) has vanished before confused alternatives. Malcolm McLaren's Duck Rock record and clothes suggest a vaguely ethnic practicality

in this suspended animation we accord the potency of wizards. Scientists, magnates, movie stars, hairdressers and athletes – anyone who has distinguished himself or herself beyond the norm has become instantly familiar within the household, and in part an arbiter of taste. These people form a constantly lengthening chain – a parallel to what we call Society – which supplies components for our own taste simply by allowing the camera to record the minutiae of each link's daily existence. This man's clothes, that one's house, this woman's hair, that one's loves, all contribute to what we think life can be or hope it is. Single figures still emerge, however, who crystallize many of these traits and make them accessible in bulk, so to speak. These new arbiters have gradually, as our century progresses, become more businessmen than creators, just as, in the early part of the century, they became more creators than aristocrats. This evolution is what we would like to make visible in this book. Our century demands, in Diaghilev's words, 'astonish me' of all who seek to profit from it. How they have done so has been lavishly recorded and widely imitated. Perhaps more than their historical antecedents, they *exist*, purely and simply. They are the visual world, and thus can change it at will. In the knowledge that any success will be greeted with the attention of the camera, these people who feel the need to change the lifestyle of our times have forged large personalities, stylized and eminently recognizable, which seem constant in every snapshot, every magazine portrait. They are thus very easily imitated. Let us look back over them and see how we have done so, and try to guess why we were astonished.

11 Montesquiou's silliness and his extreme stylistic modernity – witness the costume, predating Cardin by 60 years – marry in this photograph from his Japanese period, in the 1890s

Robert de Montesquiou
1855–1921

In the visual arts, and to some extent in life itself, the *fin-de-siècle* saw the Triumph of Literature. This is less obvious in the world of the Impressionists, where men like bank-clerks painted bank-holiday scenes in straw hats; such an art has endured as anti-literary in the popular mind. But even that milieu attracted the brilliant cosmopolitan dwarf Toulouse-Lautrec, revelled in Zola's naturalist novels, and appealed to such literary men as the brothers Goncourt or Baudelaire himself. All things for all men – women, houses, hats, not to mention politics and morals and furniture – derived in some part from either novels or histories. This was true to the extent that the Symbolist poet Stéphane Mallarmé metaphorically threw up his hands with the phrase, 'Everything in the world exists to end up in a book!' The vast influence of literature on taste originated in the combined forces of Victorian popular novels and the escapism stimulated by industrialist society. It gave rise to curious passions and impossible characters as our century began. Among these, none was more bizarre, more literary or more influential than Count Robert de Montesquiou-Fezensac. The name is now an obscure one, remembered in connection with Proust; in the history of turn-of-the-century taste it is ubiquitous.

Montesquiou inhabited a rare atmosphere and made it fashionable by the up-to-date self-promotion which was his personal reinterpretation of traditional aristocratic arrogance. Scion of an ancient family, which had survived both the Bourbons and Bonaparte ('After all, the Capets were already usurpers to us,' an ancestor remarked), he never forgot that he was a descendant of d'Artagnan. Montesquiou adapted the fourth Mousquetier's suavity and panache to Parisian salons. In his imagination he replaced the rapier thrust with the malicious epigram, Milady de Winter with the Duchesses of the Faubourg Saint-Germain, the trio of Porthos, Athos and Aramis with the painter J. A. M. Whistler, the writer Gabriele d'Annunzio and the composer Reynaldo Hahn. It is an apposite phenomenon of literature that he now survives as the model for J.-K. Huysmans's quintessential decadent hero Des Esseintes (in his best-known novel *A Rebours*) and Proust's archetypal homosexual socialite, the Baron de Charlus (in *Sodome et Gomorrhe*). The activities which set him up for these caricatures, though misinterpreted by both authors, were, in fact, those of a self-elected Professor of Beauty, an arbiter whose taste in its very capriciousness helped refocus the eye of our century and reaffirm the primacy of taste itself in the panoply of contemporary virtues.

An overly productive and mediocre poet, the Count revived the social importance of the calling by acquiring, instead of the political kudos accorded Victor-Hugo or Lamartine, a right of aesthetic veto which he exercised in matters of decoration and art. Concomitant with this high-handed attitude were a sure instinct for the new and good, and a profound, even spiritual belief in Beauty as an absolute. From these motives stemmed Montesquiou's determination to dictate style, even to artists patently beyond his sphere of influence. The amazing thing is that he did have enormous influence, rarely offending the great, who found his admiration genuine and his flattery charming. (He met his match in Whistler, one of the

few people he respected to the point of self-effacement. On the other hand, as Charlus' repeated snubs to the narrator of *Remembrance of Things Past* reveal, he easily traumatized the young Proust, whom he deeply mistrusted, perhaps sensing an incipient voyeurism in the author's attentions.) More commendably, Montesquiou bullied the rich and grand, whom he considered soulless and lacking in vision. He felt his social peers needed a deeper appreciation of the refinements of life and art, in order to combat the materialism of the *belle époque*, and that he could impart it to them. A chaste but pronounced homosexual, the count was a narcissist who sought to make the world around him a mirror of his own excellence. He was morally convinced he possessed a rare understanding of the works of man, which was both enjoyable and necessary to others; to a certain extent he was right.

Montesquiou's acts of patronage are manifold, the manner in which he patronized variable, the results too often forgotten. In his twenties he riveted the Paris of the 1880s – which expected only the most conventional behaviour from the son of the President of Society's favourite Jockey Club – by the eccentricities Huysmans exaggerated in *A Rebours*. Always physically healthy, Montesquiou nevertheless came to epitomize decadence. His reputation for morbidity was accentuated by his fastidious clothes, usually ensembles in different shades of the same colour, and the decorative conceits of the eyrie he fashioned in an attic of his father's enormous *hôtel particulier*. Here one room had walls in four shades of rose, the bathroom was hung with blue cloth surmounted by Japanese silver fishes, and the dressing-room featured vitrines where fan-shaped arrangements of socks and neckties were displayed like works of art. The flat was in fact a jumble of William Morris textiles, oriental embroideries, Japanese prints, gothic furniture and tanagra figurines. The young poet's taste was, in short, that of the Aesthetic Movement in England, but it was deployed with a unique personal allusiveness and Parisian *chic* unexampled in the more high-minded New Art homes of London or Liverpool. William Morris invented such décors for a moral reason, Montesquiou created them as another might have created a poem: to define his feelings. From this lair, he issued his magnificently-bound volumes of poetry (*Les Chauves-Souris, Les Pas Effacés* – limited editions, wrapped in silk). The count himself issued in a cape and Byronic collar to worship Sarah Bernhardt (the only woman he ever slept with) or the poet Hérédia (for this

12 (*Above left*) Montesquiou had himself photographed at every period of his life, aware of the imaginative possibilities of the camera. Here, with his secretary Gabriel d'Yturri (left), he displays a travelling costume and the manner which led him to call himself 'the Prince of Transitory Things'

13 (*Above right*) The realities of aestheticism were more robust (and dustier) than Whistler's dreamy evocations. Sarah Bernhardt surrounded herself with allusive clutter as did Montesquiou in the days when they were inseparable.

14 J. A. M. Whistler, *The Artist in his Studio*, 1864. As a young man Montesquiou responded to the minimal, so-called Japanese aesthetic created by Whistler. (*Oil on panel, 24¾ by 18¾ ins. Courtesy of the Art Institute of Chicago, Gift of the Friends of American Art*)

15 Montesquiou's own houses at Versailles and Le Vésinet greatly resembled the interior of Sargent's London studio, shown here: an eclectic fusion of contemporary clutter and period furniture evoked a dream world of aristocratic distinction

rendezvous he dressed entirely in shades of lavender grey). By thirty he had achieved a reputation for mysterious elegance and glamorous aestheticism which distinguished him among the staid dowagers of the Faubourg, and made him sought after by the 'artistic' upper-middle-class ladies of the bourgeois Plaine Monceau.

In the 1890s, as the *Prince des Odeurs Suaves* (the title of a collection of poems which he took from a character in Flaubert's *Salâmmbo* and awarded himself), Montesquiou ruled the liana-covered kingdom of *art nouveau*. He cultivated a deep friendship with the reclusive painter Gustave Moreau, to whom he presented the then uncommon bird-of-paradise flower in a gesture so memorable that the painter felt obliged to draw the plant in detail before it died. He ordered glass and furniture from the young Lalique and from Emile Gallé, with whom he corresponded on plaques of veneer in silver ink. Though he scorned Oscar Wilde (calling him 'Antinous of the Horrible'), Montesquiou made disciples among the priestesses of Sappho, very much in evidence in Paris at the turn of the century, and collected around himself a court of brilliant and sensitive young men of good family. To these refined but perverse 'souls' he gave tea in a new flat decorated with Japanese art and *art nouveau* installations, surrounded by exquisite floral arrangements from the hands of his Japanese gardener, and posing before pink or pale yellow panelling. Here his collections of Moreau, Redon and Bresdin were displayed in settings which had, for their time, a new clarity and spare elegance. The portrait of Montesquiou by Doucet shows his beauty and brooding sensitivity; another, a masterpiece, by Whistler, shows him as the arch-dandy, enveloped in the sorrowful shadows which suggest sleep and dreams. During the sittings for this portrait Whistler uttered what Montesquiou regarded as the greatest statement ever made by a painter: 'Look at me for a moment and look at yourself for ever.' Narcissism could go no further in the atmosphere of a dying century.

16 Under the influence of the Petit Trianon (built by Gabriel for Marie Antoinette), Montesquiou moved to Versailles and turned from *art nouveau* extravagance to the pursuit of eighteenth-century elegance. Public taste followed suit, and the *belle époque* began

His friendship with Whistler led to a change in Montesquiou's taste, which he demonstrated in a new house, the Palais Rose at Le Vesinet. It was here that he came into his own, achieving a status and power in the world of art which were awesome. He assembled pieces of the then-despised Empire style (which must have suggested new geometric forms of design to many artists who saw them), hung pale tinted walls with beautiful eighteenth-century frames painted white, and saved his thirst for the bizarre for the Russian Ballet and the theatrical spectacles of d'Annunzio. Indeed, one of Montesquiou's claims to fame is his part in the evolution of the strange ballet-oratorio, *The Martyrdom of St Sebastian*, composed by Debussy, written by d'Annunzio, designed by Léon Bakst, and danced by Ida Rubinstein. This forgotten masterpiece predicted the excesses of the cinema, and the mixed-media happenings of modern art, in a way even Diaghilev had not dared to do.

Hide-bound by the moral strictures of his era, Montesquiou was a lonely man. To fill his loneliness, he entertained on a scale seldom seen today. Casting his net wide, he invited the Lesbian hostess and writer Natalie Barney and her lover, the painter Romaine Brooks; he cultivated and encouraged the young composer Reynaldo Hahn, making his reputation; he snubbed the young Cocteau, but launched d'Annunzio in Paris. The autocratic arbiter of the Palais Rose has been immortalized in one of the greatest Edwardian paintings, his portrait by Boldini. It shows Montesquiou, in a silver-grey frock-coat suit, admiring the turquoise Sèvres handle of his Louis XV walking-stick. This walking-stick was a wand which Montesquiou, rich, middle-aged and at the pinnacle of a fiercely snobbish society, could wave over the upper crust, to make or break an artist's reputation. Alas, he used his power far too often in petty social vendettas, and his talents in unprintably libellous verses about the very society ladies who formed his chorus of praise.

Montesquiou loved objects, not objectively, but with a real passion. He wrote poems to

17 To understand the count's poems we need to see the details of their presentation: this silk was specially woven for the endpapers of *Les Chauves-Souris*. Such artifice added to the social prestige if not the quality of Montesquiou's verse, on which he based his claim to be a writer

18 'Everything in the world exists only to end up in a book', wrote the poet Mallarmé. For Montesquiou the book as an object, together with its poetic contents, became an end in itself

19 (*Above*) The oriental draperies and
eighteenth-century furniture jumbled in arty
juxtaposition in Sargent's Paris studio reflect
Montesquiou's taste in the 1880s. *Madame X*
in the portrait was Madame Gautreau, a
friend of the poet

20 The Comtesse Greffuhle, Montesquiou's
cousin, to whom he remained deeply attached
all his life, was the model for Proust's
Princesse de Guermantes. This photograph –
perhaps arranged by Montesquiou himself –
perfectly represents his hybrid taste: the *art
nouveau* extravagance of the dress and the
severe elegance of the Empire furniture

22 (*Above*) A younger generation, in the form of Aubrey
Beardsley, harvested the seeds of modernist daring and
dandified elegance sown by Montesquiou and his friends.
From them grew a new art and a style of wit which went far
beyond those of the inhibited aesthetes

21 (*Left*) Portrait of Montesquiou by Whistler: a figure
sadder and less graceful than his legend suggests. The poet
reported to everyone the painter's exclamation during a
sitting for this picture: 'Look at me a moment more, and
look at yourself for ever!' (*Frick Collection, New York*)

23 Boldini, the pyrotechnician of portraiture, assembled the colours, props and attitude beloved of Montesquiou's maturity in this icon of the dandy worshipping the eighteenth century – his Louis XV Sèvres-handled cane (*Musée d'Orsay, Paris*)

furniture, which sounds absurd, but which were in fact elegant and witty epigrams on the nature of style and his own taste.

> *J'aime le style Empire*
> *le pire*
> *Fait à mes yeux éblouis*
> *Mieux que le Louis XIII*
>
> I love the Empire style
> At its most vile
> It seems to my jaded eyes
> Better than Louis Treize

is not just a neatly turned phrase; it refers to the conventional pseudo-Renaissance monstrosities with which the French bourgeoisie furnished their dining-rooms up to the Second World War, and contrasts with it the hard geometric fineness of Neo-Classicism.

If such clear-cut taste may seem a curious contrast to the table-turning and spiritualist practices in which Montesquiou also indulged, let us not forget that Picasso, who reinvented Neo-Classicism for the next generation, began as a painter of hollow-cheeked souls not far from Burne-Jones' haunted figures. All these obsessions, for *art nouveau* art, antique furniture, contemporary verse and late Romantic music, share one motive: idolatry. One of the great motivations of the arbiter is an ability, even a necessity to lose himself in an

24 The Comtesse Greffuhle in the Bois de Boulogne. Anglophilia was a strong element in nineteenth-century taste, typified by English tailoring for both men (Montesquiou's sober distinction) and women (the Countess's riding habit). The Empress Elisabeth of Austria also set a fashion for this equestrian chic. It had a unisexual quality which endeared it to the traditionalist poets and tasteful ladies of the 1890s

enthusiasm, to adhere totally to an ideal. This quality and the slight melancholy, born of discontent, impatience with a stupid world, and the impotent perfectionism which accompanies it were always present in Montesquiou's life and work.

After the death in 1914 of his secretary and devoted companion, Gabriel d'Yturri (about whom Paris wits remarked viciously, 'Mort? Yturri? te salue tante', an untranslatable pun on the French argot for 'queer', which is *tante*, and the Latin *Morituri te salutant*), the Count became ever more acidulous, ever more out of step with a world which had chosen new taste-makers and discovered new styles. By the time he died (in 1921) Montesquiou was a forgotten figure as far as the public was concerned, merely a name in society columns, not one to conjure images of an elegance dimly perceived but influentially envied by the man in the street. Had he left behind him any real achievement, any great collection, any works of permanent value? Not in the way 'his' artists had, or even his contemporaries (Madame Jacquemart André, about whom he was vitriolic, left a museum of superbly electic collections

25 Rumanian by birth, the incomparable
Countess Anna de Noailles spouted quantities of
(often excellent) poetry and shared
Montesquiou's taste for a slightly false Louis
XVI style mingled with Vuillards, greyhounds,
tangos and electric light

26 Marcel Proust, here
seen emulating his idol's
profile, moustache, clothes
and furniture, saw in
Montesquiou the *sine qua
non* of artistic supremacy.
Through his long novel
Proust achieved a
comparable pinnacle for a
later generation

27 *Portrait of Whistler* by Boldini. This picture of the American painter is more suggestive of Montesquiou's waspish posing than the 'butterfly's' light arrogance. $(67\frac{1}{8} \times 37\frac{3}{16}$ *ins. Collections of the Brooklyn Museum, Gift of A. Augustus Healy)*

28 (*Above*) More than anything, the women of
Montesquiou's world reveal how completely it has vanished.
This portrait by the count's discovery and protégé Paul
Helleu of his wife was drawn in the eighteenth-century
manner: three colours of conté crayon on pale grey paper

29 (*Right*) Montesquiou and Proust loved the slithering
elegance of fabrics by the Venetian aesthete Mario Fortuny.
Here an example is modelled by Mrs Condé Nast, wife of
the first owner of *Vogue* and sister of Montesquiou's friend
Claire de Choiseul

to the city of Paris, while Edouard Commodo similarly left a marvellous museum of oriental art).

But Robert de Montesquiou was one of the hidden creators, who make life out of art. In so doing, they reflect a light around them which, perhaps inadvertently, illuminates new sensations, new shapes, and new ways of using both. He used common snobbishness to establish the poet/arbiter as a bridge between the worlds of literature, art and society – a role which Diaghilev in his day, Cocteau afterwards and fashion editors in our own have used to great advantage. He insisted that the life of the rich, unimaginably sterile in the days of his youth, should at least appear to have the spiritual bohemianism and passionate stylishness we have come to expect of what we call 'superstars'. He plucked from the chaos of nineteenth-century interior decoration elements which suited his own taste (eighteenth-century and Empire furniture, clear harmonious colours, fine bindings, beautiful rare flowers, Chinese porcelain) and made continuously novel and irresistibly elegant décors by combining them with elements of modernity (paintings by Whistler or Moreau, jewellery by Lalique, drypoints by Helleu). In these décors he led a life which made its point by a judicious if bizarre combination of accumulation and rejection. In short, he judged, and judged with a sureness that rendered his judgements, for a few years, irrefutable to a stratum of French society who generally patronized, bought, or criticized new art and the meaning of new ideas. He created no set style, but he had in his personality the precise elements of the style which was in turn 'aesthetic', *art nouveau* and historicist Edwardian; a rich and perceptive collector in all these tastes, he established a world of the spirit to which modernity as we know it (Cubism and jazz modernism in particular) were both a reaction and a reference. In this sense he created a poetry, not in words but in life, which substantiated the wish he defined in four lines of verse:

> *Je voudrais que ce vers fut un bibelot d'art*
> *Spécial, curieux, particulier, étrange;*
> *Avec, sur son pourtour, quelquefois un regard*
> *De couleur bizarre et qui dérange.*

> An art knick-knack of verse I want to make
> (Rare or curious, important or bad)
> With sometimes on its surface just a flake
> Of some strange colour that will drive you mad.

30 Impresario, socialite and aesthetic gambler, Sergei Diaghilev found a spiritual home in the Principality of Monaco, where the Ballets Russes were based in the years following World War I. Here he strolls in Monte Carlo, half Russian prince, half comedian

Sergei Diaghilev
1872–1929

Today barbarianism has a recognized place in the arts. Novelty is almost inextricably tangled with shock value, and the purpose of the artist is, to a great extent, cathartic. This concept is a novel one, developed throughout our century, and breaking with the art of the past. Academies were not always despised tribunals; Royal Europe and Imperial Russia, throughout the nineteenth century, were proud of the grandiose official art of the times. In the 1880s, when Symbolism emerged from late Romanticism, it was to this other-worldly, preeminently aristocratic art that connoisseurs looked for stimulus, not to the realist revolution posterity has decided was quintessential to the era. This attitude, a form of aesthetic legitimacy corresponding to dynastic loyalties, broke down under many diverse influences, vanishing entirely with the First World War. However, like all revolutions, the demise of traditional values in the arts began, so to speak, in a palace, and was led by a princely nonconformist. Tsarist Absolutism was uniquely applied to modernist spectacle in the travelling circus known throughout the world as *Les Ballets Russes*; its ring-master, Sergei Diaghilev, was the first of the Barbarians.

Born in the same year as Aubrey Beardsley and Max Beerbohm (1872), though in less obscure circumstances, Diaghilev was part of the complex minor aristocracy of the Romanov Empire, a world of wealthy civil servants and soldiers, each a cog turning in its appointed place within the obsolescent social machine which finally ceased to function in 1917. Diaghilev, on close inspection, had a double inheritance: on the one hand, the benefits of a secure, affluent and intellectual background, on the other, the insecurity of a perceptive mind developing during times of change and unrest. His psychological constitution was similarly split, confident in its taste, knowledge and overbearing sense of authority, but troubled and compulsive about the imagined personality of his mother (who died giving him birth) and his conspicuous homosexuality. There may have been many men in *fin-de-siècle* Russia with such a symbolic relation to their times, but few if any were so self-aware or made such startling use of their contradictory impulses.

Diaghilev emerged from his musical, bookish protected childhood on family estates near Perm, a provincial capital, as a burly young man with an unworldly charm. Enrolled as a law student in St Petersburg (like many young men of good family with little interest in jurisprudence), he nurtured ambitions as a composer, which he pursued lackadaisically while staying with his cousin Dima Filosofov. Dima was the aesthete of the family, part of a group of nostalgic artists, writers and connoisseurs which included Alexandre Benois, Léon Bakst and the Baron de Gunzbourg. Diaghilev initially made a poor impression on this energetic creative circle, but it was the bearish young composer of bad piano pieces who would carry the *cénacle*'s ideas to Western Europe, and change modern art in the process.

Blossoming in the congenial atmosphere provided by this group, stimulated by the grandiose beauties of Imperial Petersburg, accepting with grace the failure of his musical ambitions (Rimsky-Korsakov himself dismissed them outright), Diaghilev came to some very mature conclusions about himself, which he listed in a letter to his beloved stepmother:

31 (*Above*) Léon Bakst created this lavishly coloured set for Diaghilev's production of *Schéhérazade*: his colours set new fashions, splashing over dresses, textiles, furniture and even architecture. Orientalism became so much the rage that Diaghilev was later obliged to counter it with new ballets

32 (*Left*) Nijinsky in *Le Dieu Bleu*, 1913. When Diaghilev grew more and more daring in his modernism he left behind the bejewelled spectacles of Bakst. This coincided with the end of his affair with Nijinsky, the Blue God of Cocteau's mediocre ballet

33 (*Right*) Such was Paul Poiret's success that fashionable women left his salon convinced they were sultanas or slaves, referring to the couturier as 'le magnifique'. Diaghilev thus saw his patronesses transformed into reflections of his dancers

34 The harem scene from *Schéhérazade* suggested a range of costume, lighting and pose soon emulated by sophisticated people off stage

I am first a great charlatan, though with brio; secondly a great charmer; thirdly, I have any amount of cheek; fourthly, I am a man with a great quantity of logic, but with very few principles; fifthly, I think I have no real gifts. All the same, I think I have just found my true vocation – being a Maecenas. I have all that is necessary, save the money – *mais ça viendra*.

Few arbiters of elegance have ever categorized the prerequisites of their status so accurately. In recognizing these characteristics as components of *action* Diaghilev knowingly established the role of patron in a new framework. His mention of money removes his aesthetics from the aristocratic pedestal of previous taste-makers and, in making them marketable, predicts the business of the new which he helped to make an industry.

Ballet, with which Diaghilev's name is instantly associated today, was not the first art to which he applied his mind. Benois was an elegant draughtsman, dedicated to imagining eighteenth-century life in Peter the Great's capital; Bakst, a more ebullient modernist, was a designer of distinction, passionately interested in costume and décor; Diaghilev shared with both men a fervid enthusiasm for the new in art, nostalgic elegance and – most originally – an inspired fusion of the two. He began to collect pictures, toured Europe to look at museums and ateliers (as well as assiduously developing the social connections which would prove to be mainstays of his future enterprises), and cultivated the fashionable tone which the period demanded of its artistic advisers. In 1897 he organized an exhibition of German and English watercolours, exquisitely arranged; Scandinavian art, Finnish and Russian contemporary works, international Impressionist painting were all promoted by this cultural Prometheus in large-scale public exhibitions with official backing. Coincidentally, in 1898, Diaghilev convinced private collectors that they should back a seminal magazine called *The World of Art* (*Mir Iskusstva*), which proved to be a dossier of ideas and interests cultivated by his circle of friends: Beardsley appeared in it (Diaghilev, on the recommendation of Oscar Wilde, had met the artist shortly before his death), as did Charles Rennie Mackintosh, the Scottish *art nouveau* architect, Gustave Moreau, the Symbolist painter, and Anton Vrubel, the peculiar genius of Russian Symbolism, who painted the subjects of Moreau in the manner of Cézanne. All these discoveries, together with unearthings from Russian art history (the architecture of Rastrelli, ikon painting, national arts and crafts) were presented in a luxurious and original

35 In the Théâtre Royal at Monte Carlo Diaghilev presented many of his ballets. The gilt ceilings (by Garnier, architect of the Paris Opéra) and pseudo-Louis XIV grandeur may well have contributed to *The Sleeping Beauty* and other similar productions

format, using special typefaces and fine papers. With the magazine as his manifesto, Diaghilev's name reached a wide audience among the educated classes, and allowed him to capitalize on a reputation for charm, industry and enthusiasm. There were, however, cracks in this somewhat precious façade, which eventually led to a dramatic rupture with his homeland and his own taste.

Although *The World of Art* also led to an appointment as editor of the Imperial Theatre annual (which was turned into a similarly de luxe publication), Diaghilev's extravagance, obvious homosexuality and tactless proselytizing for his friends (which came to the fore when he was commissioned to oversee a new production of Délibes's ballet *Sylvia*) led to a crisis. Although his efforts had thus far gained notice and approval from the Tsar and his family, Diaghilev's attempts to oppose the Theatre bureaucracy (an organized civil service in Russia) with string-pulling cost him his job. This sequence of obstinate innovation, conservative backlash, intrigue and *folie de grandeur* was something Diaghilev carried into his future life. Partly the result of his autocratic manner (more effective outside the country where he was only an untitled aesthete), and partly a result of the establishment's real horror of novelty, these explosions became the impresario's litmus test for success. Years later, when a composer wondered if he would have preferred his ballet to have had a violent reception like Stravinsky's *Sacre du Printemps*, Diaghilev knowingly remarked, 'It's not as easy as you think.'

The *Sylvia* affair must have left Diaghilev with a score to settle in relation to the ballet, but he turned his attention once more to painting and to the opera. A huge and sumptuous

36 The couturier Poiret took up the stimulus of
Russian exoticism to develop glittering modes
like this cape-coat, 1926, for the rich Parisiennes
he had freed from corsetry. The drawings are by
Dufy

37 (*Right*) Ida Rubinstein as Cleopatra. The
'mysterious East' explored in Diaghilev's
ballets lent its aura to dressmaking, design,
even perfumery: 'L'heure bleue' or 'Shalimar'
still preserve whiffs of Edwardian naughtiness

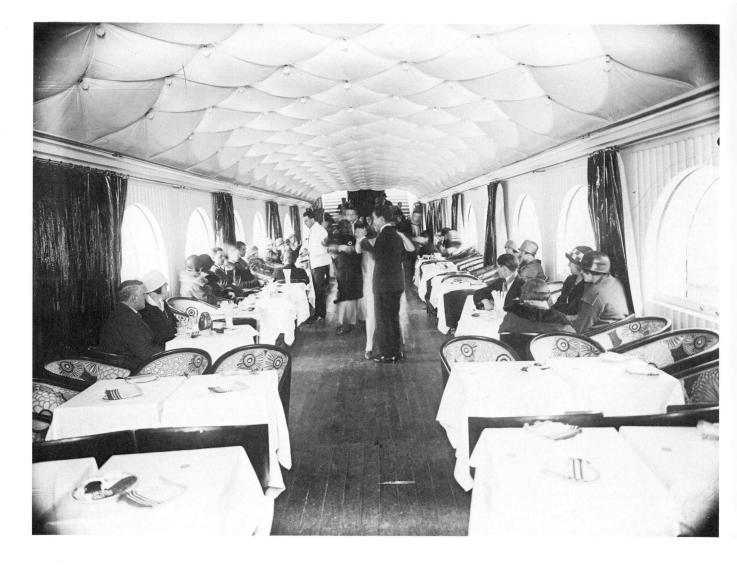

exhibition of Russian portraits through the centuries somewhat restored his credit at home; it also travelled to Paris, Berlin and Vienna. In 1905 and 1907 Diaghilev organized concerts of Russian music in Paris; in 1908 he took Mussorgsky's *Boris Godunov* to the Paris Opéra and scored a colossal success. Imperial patronage had been restored to him for promoting national interests abroad so effectively; the Grand Duke Vladimir (Nicholas II's uncle) sponsored the cultural exports; Chaliapin, the great bass, and the composers Glazunov, Rachmaninov, and Rimsky-Korsakov triumphed in these seasons, creating a popular demand for all things Russian. In 1909 Benois suggested adding ballet to the new repertoire, pointing out that the classical Russian school of dance was unknown in France, where the discipline only survived in a debased Romantic tradition. Intrigue began again, however, with this new element. Duke Vladimir died, and his mistress, the great dancer Mathilde Kchessinskaya, withdrew from roles assigned her. Diaghilev responded to the coincidental financial disaster by making the ballet more important than the opera in his season, and finding private patronage to subsidize it.

It is only against these complex social and monetary confusions that the emergence of a new taste in European art can be seen. Behind the legendary première of the *Saison Russe* at the Opéra in May 1909 lay not only the ponderous small-mindedness of anachronistic Tsarist bureaucracy, but an essentially revolutionary attitude on the part of young composers, artists, choreographers, and Diaghilev himself. In supporting his own tastes, Diaghilev chose to be Emperor of the New, rather than Majordomo to the Classical. This aggressive stance was a novel one for an *arbiter elegantiarum*. It raised him to the position of autocrat, and the elegancies to art forms.

The first night, which included an eighteenth-century fantasia on a book by Benois, *Le Pavillon d'Armide*, and the compellingly blood-curdling Polovtsian dances from *Prince Igor*, encapsulated – in the former – the nostalgic aspect of Diaghilev's taste, and – in the latter – his taste for shock tactics. Both captured the imagination of the cultured world, which, each

38 The restaurant of Poiret's barge, with its fat *Biedermeier* chairs and Empire tented ceiling, shows the influence of Diaghilev's nineteenth-century nostalgia: here modernism was close to pastiche

39 The taste for jungles, cushions and low couches promoted by Poiret ranged across Europe, achieving a cluttered vulgarity against which Diaghilev instinctively reacted

40 In Poiret's décor for
his houseboat exhibition at
the 1925 World's Fair he
linked French cabinet-
making with the cushions
of *Schéhérazade*

41 Another interior
concocted by Poiret's
design atelier 'Martine'
shows the origins of *art
déco* in Russian luxury

42 Nijinsky by J.-E. Blanche. This dancer, whom Diaghilev loved, personified the sensual grace and exoticism which he flung into the stately stream of the *belle époque*. The coromandel screen and Turkish carpet suggest that Blanche, in common with many other artists, was already in the grip of Orientalism

year until 1929, waited eagerly for the impresario's next revolution. The succession of novelties Diaghilev flung at the public in the form of ballets is too long to list. A few components – *Schéhérazade, Petroushka, Parade, Apollon Musagète, Ode, Le Train Bleu* – will suggest the range of style with which Diaghilev overrode his own tastes in favour of effective contrasts. Artists such as the Russian cubist Larionov, Mechanists Gabo and Pevsner, Picasso in two different styles, the neo-Romantic Tchelitchew, or fashionable Dufy supplanted the exoticism of Bakst and Benois, reflecting his changing enthusiasms, providing new settings for the talents he nurtured: Nijinsky, Karsavina, Lifar, Balanchine. Diaghilev collected styles the way other people collected pictures or books (indeed, when undiagnosed diabetes and emotional strain affected him to the point where he proposed to disband the company, the cardinal sign of his apparent change of interest was a manic concentration on collecting rare and beautiful books).

However, the exotic style for which Diaghilev was most specifically the catalyst was one which he himself eventually felt the need to refute in favour of the post-Picasso décors ornamenting his ballets during the Twenties. The contradiction was necessitated by the very success of his first wave of productions in the oriental genre, which swept a riot of colour and sumptuousness into the pale grey drawing-rooms of the Edwardian *beau monde* and repeated for the twentieth century the escapist *chinoiserie* of the eighteenth. *Schéhérazade, Cléopâtre, Le Dieu Bleu* (Cocteau's attempt to cash in on the already fading genre in 1912) or the first *Firebird* production all conformed to a formula combining cushions, crimson paint, feathers, ropes of pearls, harem trousers and an indefinable eroticism, parodied in silent films like Valentino's *The Sheik* or Theda Bara's *Cleopatra*. It is this lodestar East which caught the public imagination, paving the way for furniture by Carlo Bugatti, Jacques-Emile Ruhlmann and Eileen Gray, making a demand for literature like Elinor Glyn's *Three Weeks* or *The Garden of Allah*, and paralleling the fashion revolution of Paul Poiret, a Parisian Diaghilev, who freed women from corsets and draped them in the costumes of the Russian Ballet. The actual stylistic details of this brief pre-war period (which survived into the early Twenties) have been the subject of many publications; it is the psychological drama surrounding Diaghilev which throws him into relief as a real *arbiter*, a transmitter of new ideas beyond his conscious promotions.

We owe the concept of the autocrat in public entertainment to Diaghilev; instead of regarding him as a political figure, the public learned to accept the aristocrat as a showman, a new decorative role for a vanishing breed. With the character went elements of perversity, shady or high-handed behaviour and extravagance which to this day we find riveting in anecdotes about impresarios, publishing magnates and great art dealers. Homosexuality itself assumed a sort of glamour in the world which elevated Nijinsky to the level of a deity; in the same way the productions of otherwise controversial avant-garde artists were accepted for their entertainment value rather than their polemical aesthetics. Here is the hub of Russian Ballet exoticism: it seduced, even through the medium of scandal, caressing the eye and ear in a way which made modernism seductive, setting a precedent for the so-called revolutions in the world of art. The amorphous creativity of Pop Art, for instance, with its multi-media events, glittering icons and personality cults would not have been possible without the communal memory of Diaghilev's equally unhinged milieu.

Exhibitionism, previously the domain of music-hall artistes and dandies, became respectable with the advent of the Russian Ballet, especially for women. The entire concept of the star, male or female, who behaved like royalty was carefully cultivated by Diaghilev – who

43 Duncan Grant's studio at Charleston. Half Montparnasse, half St Petersburg, the Bloomsbury group borrowed modernism and Orientalism from Diaghilev. The Omega Workshops crudely applied the Ballets Russes styles in a technically inferior echo of Poiret's creations

44 Once unleashed, the stream of fashionable exoticism derived from Diaghilev's spectacles extended as far as Hollywood. The nascent star system chose Rudolf Valentino as the Nijinsky of the silver screen; in *The Sheik* Bakst's draperies and Fokine's choreography of *Schéhérazade* were dimly reflected

45 (*Right*) The bizarre tableaux of the Nijinsky/Debussy ballet *L'après-midi d'un faune* created scandals and a new vein of neo-classicism in the world of art; from this work derived the sculptures of Bourdelle, the clothes of Madame Vionnet, and much of Cocteau's 'Greek' aesthetic

obviously felt an inner need to dominate the arts by ukase, perpetuating the annual creation of new cult-figures as an enviable Tsar system. The homosexual's enthusiasm for women of decorative allure led him to confer on Karsavina, Rubinstein or Lopokova a status that protected him from their love but made them his puppets; the same thing held more dramatically true with his male dancers, whom he owned and would not free. The amateur, of which Ida Rubinstein was the supreme example, could assume an elevated position in this world, on the strength of aesthetic appeal. This platonic *amour des yeux* has persisted in the world of art, elevating to a higher sphere the basic human need for pin-ups or caricatures. The history of Hollywood, the system of Notables in American politics, and the overnight idolatries of the rock music scene all derive from the elective absolutism of popular taste which began with Diaghilev's 1909 season in Paris. This is why the late 1960s saw such a revival of interest in the Ballets Russes and their times; history is repeating itself faster and faster in our century, and the Barbarian Aristocrat is one of our archetypes. His importance is

46 (*Left*) Pablo Picasso. Cocteau's real contribution to the Ballets Russes was a link with Montparnasse, Picasso and revolutionary avant-garde art. In this conjunction lay Diaghilev's future

47 In Schumann's *Carnaval* Diaghilev presented Romance as historicism. His designers delighted to dress Tamara Karsavina in the appropriate fashions of the 1830s, which, later, combined with popular Orientalism in some decorative Twenties styles

not just in the history of ballet. Of course he put ballet on the map of Western culture; but he also made a place for the exile, anticipated the glamour of the Russian fugitive from Philistinism, and, in his somewhat sad splendour, represented that class of taste-maker elected by the purchasing public without which art itself might not have survived the holocausts of our times.

Lady Mendl (Elsie de Wolfe) 1865–1950

Elsie Mendl [signature]

Like Pushkin's Queen of Spades, Lady Mendl, who began life as an impoverished climber on the slopes of New York society, seemed to have gained, at a terrible price, the secrets of winning at cards and of longevity, growing richer, older and better-looking throughout the years from 1890 to 1940. Her very presence became a legend, providing a beacon to social climbers and collectors the world over. This phenomenal if trivial life represents a subtle and important shift in the elements of taste. It was lived by a woman doing a man's job and using taste as a spearhead in the attack on a society whose approval she had reason to doubt. Characteristic hard-headedness, super-snobbery, and an exaggerated respect for the minutiae of life resulted from this change, habits which came quickly to replace the weapons of previous arbiters: authority, aristocracy and amateurishness.

Elsie de Wolfe was born with a chip on her shoulder. The de Wolfe family were a pedigreed one in New England, but without the fortune more essential to nineteenth-century prominence than an old Dutch name. A lantern jaw and bushy eyebrows added to the young woman's sense of unease, which was fuelled by a burning desire to shine among the stars of the *status quo*. Native wit and a brave resourcefulness led her to a remedy for her social position which caused the first ripples of gossip around a life spent in the limelight for another sixty years: she 'went on the stage'. Today such a step would cause no surprise, but in 1885 it was not the expected follow-up to years of continental 'finishing' (even if four of them took place in a Scots parsonage) or of presentation at the court of Queen Victoria. However, amateur glamour was, to Miss de Wolfe, better than no glamour at all; in her case it was a great deal better. She had somehow contrived, during her year in London, to make friends with the former New Orlenian Mrs Brown Potter, herself no mean drawing-room mime, who had presented Elsie in private performances before audiences including the Prince of Wales. With such cachet, Elsie could go far in the raw atmosphere of New York elitism.

Her various performances culminated in the opening week of New York's luxurious country club, Tuxedo Park (1887). Appearing at that event, she assisted at the invention of the Tuxedo jacket, the debut of a woman eventually to become America's Chesterfield, Emily Post, and the first success of that sprawl of country clubs which would dominate American social life until the Second World War. All those elements, and the wealth that supported them, were grist to Elsie's mill. Something more important was the relationship she began as a result of that performance with an already portly, bossy and definitely unglamorous woman named Elizabeth Marbury.

To modern eyes an obvious lesbian, 'Bessie' was to her contemporaries a woman who carried forthright, mannish speech and behaviour to a point that was only protected from disparaging analysis by the naïveté of the era, and her secure place in New York's moneyed Brownstone upper crust. This position was sufficiently pre-eminent for Miss Marbury not to need to exercise it in any frivolous way: she dismissed Paris gowns and parties as fripperies; cultivating chickens and studying modern science seemed admirable alternatives to her – at least until she met Miss de Wolfe, the much-talked-about 'Queen of the Amateur Stage'.

48 Virtually creating the career of 'interior decorator', Lady Mendl made and spent many fortunes in a long life which took her from suburban New York to Paris and Hollywood

The two women responded immediately to each other: Bessie to Elsie's frenchified polish (or 'chic' as it came to be called in the 1890s); Elsie to Bessie's solid protectiveness and professionalism. Indeed, this last quality was perhaps the strongest bond in their long relationship. Both obviously realized a need for intense professionalism as an antidote to the wifely status expected of women at that time, and both pursued the freedom and power such an attitude could grant for the rest of their lives. Miss Marbury became a play-broker, in fact she all but reinvented the profession, representing major European authors, as well as American ones, and securing hithertofore elusive American rights which proved so profitable to playwrights like Oscar Wilde, A. W. Pinero, or Henri Bernstein. Was this the influence of the soubrette with whom she lived? Probably, because Elsie too went professional during the last decade of the century, finding real success as an elegant clothes-horse in such nostalgic productions as *Thermidor* (a picture of Directoire Paris created by Charles Frohman). The two women shared an historic home, Irving House, on New York's Lower East Side. Foretastes of her later life were a feature of this period: the magnificence of her stage costumes for *Thermidor* elicited comment from United States customs officers, who were later to level so much duty on antiques which she attempted to import at low estimates that she decided (in 1919) to live permanently in France; meanwhile, her transformation of Washington Irving's unassuming house would lead directly to the creation of the career at which she triumphed.

At this point in Elsie de Wolfe's long life it is worth noting the elements of a mind which dealt so forcefully with matters of taste throughout the century. She was no connoisseur, in

49 The Mendls' penthouse apartment in Paris. Classic 'decorator' enthusiasms, even today, derive from Elsie's refined, unstartling preferences for French furniture, lavish upholstery and unobtrusive works of art

50 The American stage launched Elsie's social
career. She made a reputation for style in
costume pieces like *Thermidor*; this reputation she
transmuted into an authoritative position on
matters of taste

51 Influenced by Robert de Montesquiou, Elsie and her friends Elizabeth Marbury and Anne Morgan purchased the Villa Trianon at Versailles. Extensive redecoration of the old house established Elsie's taste in Paris

52 Like the Windsors, Elsie travelled with countless expensive steamer trunks from Vuitton, the Paris firm which had made luggage for the Empress Eugénie. Her world focused on the particulars of luxury as components of style

the Berensonian sense; Elsie knew quality because she read about it, and brought to its recognition a sense of line and shape. Beyond that point her taste was undeveloped. She preferred furniture to pictures, and second-rate decorative pictures to great ones. Her years on the stage formed in her a sense of the importance of her surroundings; she used her carefully prepared backgrounds to underline the show of normal femininity, social grandeur and moneyed ease essential to the eminence for which she thirsted. Literate, but not intellectual, she inherited a tough New England sense of thrift, which years of pecuniary dissimulation converted into brass-tacks business acumen. Many moves as a child whose family was haunted by financial ruin gave her an easy ability, almost a compulsion, to decorate and abandon a chosen home, while her concealed but apparently satisfying life with Miss Marbury lent her a basic security that enabled Elsie to keep up the appearance of a free agent. In short, curious, perhaps uniquely American accidents of place and time made Elsie de Wolfe an eternal *ingénue*, a potential tycoon, and an egomaniac fortunately endowed with a sense of beauty prerequisite to pronouncing on life 'as it should be'. When one adds to these characteristics the awesome circle of connections and financial backing surrounding Elizabeth Marbury (and Anne Morgan, the great financier J. Pierpont's daughter, with whom the two ladies formed a friendly triumvirate called 'the Bachelors'), it is easy to see just how potent a career might await the dissatisfied minor actress at the turn of the century.

With Bessie's funds, Elsie swept away the comfortable clutter which the two of them had accumulated at Irving House, replacing it with striped wallpaper, white-painted Louis XVI (-ish) furniture, good Turkey carpets and light-coloured curtains. The aim was a fresh elegance akin to the refined sparsity she had learned to appreciate in the house of her new

53 In the 1930s Elsie de Wolfe had become Lady Mendl. Through cosmetic surgery, exercise and sheer bravado she achieved a fragile youthfulness which matched her de luxe taste in interior decoration

54 (*Right*) Elsie promoted her friends, suggesting Spanish painter José Maria Sert (here with his wife) for the Goya pastiches which decorated the ballroom of the New York Waldorf Astoria

55 (*Above*) Coco Chanel. In the public mind, Elsie's grand style became linked with success and social climbing. In Chanel's Place Vendôme apartment the same luxurious eclecticism prevailed until the 1960s

56 (*Left*) Freeloading party-giver Elsa Maxwell, here as an Indian potentate at a ball in New York, masterminded much of Elsie's social life. Her rampant snobbery appealed to the insecure aristocracy of post-war Europe in much the same way as Elsie's arrogant savoir-faire

friend, Comte Robert de Montesquiou. Elsie and Bessie, with Anne Morgan, sojourned regularly in France, acquiring before 1900 the Villa Trianon at Versailles, where Montesquiou also lived. 'Minna', Marchioness of Anglesey, also an American, guided their first steps into international society, and shared her own passionate interest in antiques with the Bachelors. Such heady company, together with the finesse of French living and her own ambitions, lent a new impetus to Elsie's concept of self; more and more confident in her taste, she refurbished, refurnished, and reanimated the Villa Trianon, making of it the perfect setting for entertaining a disparate crew of artists, aesthetes and aristocracy which gave her pleasure and Bessie clients.

In 1905, with the encouragement of many New York ladies, and the backing of her own Sapphic friends, she sent out discreet cards, marked with a small wolf's head and a flower, which announced the availability of her services in decorating the home. The career of Interior Decorator was born with this gesture, and Elsie de Wolfe set the tone for all its future practitioners.

After various smaller domestic commissions, the newly-founded Colony Club, a ladies' sanctum conceived as a well-to-do feminist counterpart to established male conclaves, invited her to execute its décor. The result was a triumph, celebrating the values of fine old furniture, spaciousness, graciousness and chintz, a fabric Elsie used so lavishly that for many years she was called 'The Chintz Lady'. Her success, both financial and professional, was a remarkable achievement for a pre-First World War single woman; Elsie privately savoured her satisfaction to the full. She developed a shrewd nose for acquiring pieces which she could sell at increased prices to clients; she maintained the ladylike grandeur she felt suitable to her position, and attacked with confidence such apparently hopeless institutions as the brownstone or the small city apartment. Both of these dismal types of dwellings she converted into models of cosmopolitan niceness, with great good sense, a lot of good furniture, and some good works of art. Naturally, she sold each example for a handsome profit.

The Villa Trianon continued to be the real love of Elsie's life. Up until the outbreak of the First World War, she visited it every summer, lavishing whim and fortune on it as though it were a mistress. It contained no masterpieces (a collection of drawings by the witty eighteenth-century silhouettist Carmontelle was of less value in those days than now), no architectural distinction (wings added as the years passed were apposite but undistinguished, no competition for the gem-like music pavilion erected in the garden), and no important history (indeed, the many private bathrooms, steam heating and modern household offices were a modernistic scandal to local builders) – but it had charm, and that, in the long run, was what Elsie was after.

After distinguished service in the Ambulance Corps during the War, Elsie received the Croix de Guerre and moved to France; Bessie stayed in New York; Anne Morgan also remained in America, turning her attention to the suffragette issues at which she excelled. Elsie added to her possessions a flat in Paris (centring, curiously, on a mirrored bathroom which can be said to have invented the style of the Twenties, with its painted reflecting glass, low coffee-tables and air of luxurious informality).

Increasingly on her own, she became a renowned hostess among the international expatriates who included the Cole Porters, the young Cecil Beaton, the Hon. Mrs Reginald Fellowes, and a host of minor aristocrats. Simultaneously Elsie, forever darting across the world to execute commissions, grew younger: always fit, and a vegetarian, she became exaggeratedly thin, dyed her sparse hair with the first blue rinses, and made startling

57 Christian Dior. In his rococo-Victorian Paris house the taste established by Lady Mendl as appropriate to worldly success survived into post-World-War-II Paris

58 (*Right*) Elsie advised the newly-married Duchess of Windsor on the furnishings of her French house. Taste and commercialism mingled as thoroughly as object and personality in this photograph of Elsie's fellow American

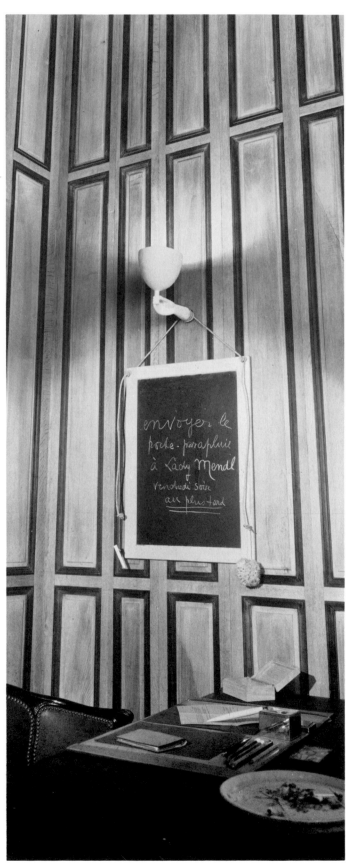

59 (*Above*) A *mariage blanche* with the British honorary attaché in Paris Sir Charles Mendl gave Elsie the title her personal sense of grandeur demanded, as well as marking a new youth for the sixty-year-old flapper

60 (*Right*) A note *à propos* Lady Mendl presides over the elegant, half-Surrealist, half-Louis XVI office of the fashionable 1930s decorator Jean-Michel Frank: by that time Elsie was acknowledged dowager empress of the profession

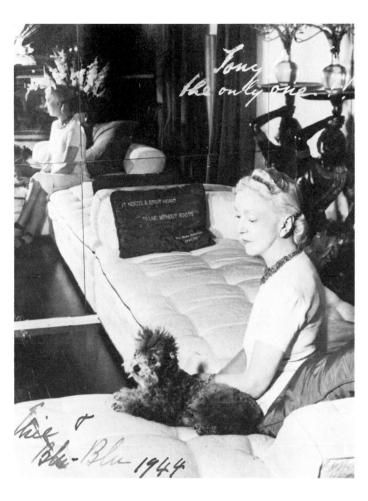

61 In her seventies, her hair dyed baby-blue to match her poodle, Elsie reigned over an increasingly middle class court in America, where she supported a lavish life-style with shrewd freebooting and publicity

appearances on the Venetian Lido with a gym instructor, who put her through dislocation exercises. As she entered her sixties, she appeared a tough little girl, wearing her trademark tiny white gloves, ruling an international world of gracious living with a rod of iron (which she probably bought at Cartier's).

Of all our century's arbiters of elegance, Elsie probably left a more definite heritage than any other: no superb collection, no trend-setting discoveries among bohemian artists, no political applications of taste, but rather the whole concept of Taste as a career. When she proposed a marriage of convenience to Sir Charles Mendl, who was loosely attached to the British Embassy in Paris, Elsie acquired the ultimate sanction for her own sense of discrimination: in 1926 she became Lady Mendl, a distinction which reinforced the esteem of those exclusive clients who asked her to 'fix up' their houses or villas, and more than doubled her price scale. This grand position, not supported by a flair for art itself, but by a sense of the appropriate background for the rich of all sorts and nations, was the precedent for decorators from Syrie Maugham (Somerset's maligned wife, who launched all-white décors in the 1930s) to David Hicks. The combination of French or English furniture, decorative but non-aggressive pictures, and expensive upholstery and fittings has remained the *sine qua non* of millionaires and would-be millionaires since the year Elsie created it. It is appropriate that Lady Mendl inhabited the Villa Trianon, for her costly good taste has become, for our times, like the nearby farm at the Trianon where Marie Antoinette escaped her duties in a pastoral charade. Similar fecklessness led the Duke and Duchess of Windsor to refer to themselves as

62 In Hollywood in the 1940s, cut off from her French milieu, Elsie exaggerated her own style with poor-quality 'Frenchy' furniture and frivolous knick-knacks to create a style that remained popular in Tinsel Town throughout the Fifties

64 (*Right*) In America and England Elsie's *dicta* about decorating with 'good pieces' and 'matching colours' turned gradually into a vapid traditionalism still popular today

63 (*Right*) Desk by Tony Duquette for Elsie's Beverly Hills house. The young Duquette, a flamboyant and imaginative cabinet-maker, was Elsie's discovery and *cavaliere servente* in Los Angeles

65 Painted by Boldini in the early 1890s (she cut off the head and framed it, disapproving of his writhing figuration), Elsie lived into her mid–eighties, smug, tidy and tenacious

Darby and Joan, he professing he would rather have been a stockbroker, and she a housewife. Elsie, naturally, advised them on the arrangement of their various Paris houses, and their country place, the Moulin de la Tuilerie. Without this example of power achieved by the peddling of elegant but unintellectual *luxe, calme et volupté*, the careers of Billy Baldwin, doyen of American interior designers (a euphemism Elsie would have approved of) or even Cecil Beaton would have been unimaginable. She took Taste into the market-place, without, ironically, losing any of its social cachet, but increasing its financial rewards and inflating its pretentiousness.

When she died in Beverly Hills in 1950, Elsie was in her mid-eighties; face-lifted, jewel-hung, spruce and up-to-date, she remained the personification of that compulsive femininity which is typical of so many rich American women. Inventor of one of the century's most lucrative professions, she left behind her an image of originality and novelty that, on close analysis, amounts to what is now a very sought-after quality – marketable charm.

66 The Duquette *papier-mâché* baroque pieces in Elsie's house suited southern California frivolity. As a result of her tyrannical patronage he went on to a distinguished design career

67 Georgia O'Keeffe and Alfred Stieglitz were married, but, with typical graciousness, he sacrificed himself to her need for solitude and open space, which she eventually satisfied by building a life of her own in the Southwest

Alfred Stieglitz
1864–1946

In 1884 Alfred Stieglitz, studying in Germany, was twenty years old. The preceding two decades which, in Europe, saw the end of Napoleon III's glittering if meretricious Second Empire, and the rise of the Arts and Crafts Movement in England, were, for Americans, the turbulent epoch of the Civil War and its confused aftermath. The liberal Eastern States, where industry was based, saw meteoric fortunes made and lost during the late 1860s and 1870s; the affluent commercialism of the 1850s gave way to a sober worship of finance where Astors, Goulds or Vanderbilts were established as national deities; a frumpy toneless domestic taste, represented by New York City's rows of brownstone town-houses, rapidly evolved to suit this period of puritan acumen. The ranks of investors and speculators on the stock-market changed from a society of flashy *arrivistes* to a black-clad militia of defenders of the national economy. Culture was not a subject of public interest or debate, but a home-charm, reserved for fireside appreciation or official demonstration through bequests to new museums or old universities.

Stieglitz's father, born in Germany, abandoned an intellectual calling for trade, first in mathematical instruments, then the woollen industry. He prospered, married Hedwig Werner, another German, and raised his children in an atmosphere of open-minded curiosity far removed from the hide-bound provincialism of his fellow-countrymen. Alfred Stieglitz thus benefited from the financial security available to the unmoneyed middle classes during the 1870s, as well as the bourgeois liberalism and intellectual distinction which had belonged to his father's Germany in the 1840s. These two traits are evident throughout his career as an American taste-maker. Stieglitz's hybrid heredity bestowed uniquely American benefits which constituted his democratic attitude towards the arts.

Stieglitz's importance as an arbiter lies in this democracy. It is not so much that he exhibited Picasso, Duchamp or Brancusi *in* America, as that he exhibited them *for* Americans that made his personal effect a unique one. Although his interests, both as photographer and gallery-owner, appeared esoteric and cultist at the time, they can, in retrospect, be viewed as extraordinarily unprejudiced and all-embracing. He truly desired the new in art; he sought it diligently, responded when it arrived, and presented it with no frills. He combined this presentation with hard-headed business sense, creating a market for work he believed in, rightly assuming that his compatriots would not believe in it too unless they had paid for it. With this achievement went the subtler distinction of launching a woman artist, Georgia O'Keeffe, for reasons which, to begin with, were concerned entirely with her talent, point of view and original technique. In a decade which looked upon Stieglitz's promotions as odd enough without a feminist overtone, this discovery of O'Keeffe seemed an even greater eccentricity, and one which left his private life open to public scrutiny. That he could convert the public to the works of this very difficult woman, on the grounds that her art was good, the lady was an all-American talent, and the paintings were increasing in value, augured well for the entire art trade in the United States. He stayed with her even when O'Keeffe's artistic pursuits led her into a solitude which increasingly excluded him, and this reflects magnifi-

68 (*Left*) The austere symbolic grandeur of Edward Gordon Craig's stage sets no doubt left an impression on Stieglitz's memory. This sensitive portrait of the designer by the young photographer Eduard Steichen, one of Stieglitz's artists, records the links between the European avant-garde and American intellectuals

69 (*Right*) *The Steerage*, photograph by Stieglitz. 'Your tired, your poor, your toiling masses' sought in America freedom and new life. All his life Stieglitz believed the freshest modern art could provide those vital qualities

cently on those loyalties and appreciations he had inherited from nineteenth-century German culture. Whatever personal psychology motivated him it is as a looker, a doer and a seller – all parts of America's best version of the pursuit of happiness – that Stieglitz made a niche in the history of taste far removed from those of his European contemporaries.

With a relaxed decisiveness uncommon among dollar-multiplying New York business-men, Stieglitz's father retired in 1881, feeling he had made enough money, and took his family to Europe for a little 'finishing'. After the grand tour, Alfred was settled in Berlin to study physics. This led, through ineptitude at higher mathematics, to a course in photo-chemistry, which led in turn to photography. Supported by a generous allowance, Alfred experimented with the camera (at first behind a door in his boarding-house room, which folded against the wall to make a tiny darkroom in a corner). By 1885 his results were published in German periodicals, and in 1887 he won a first prize from the *Amateur Photographer*, a London magazine, in a contest.

Photography developed rapidly during this period, influencing the art of the Impressionist painters in France, and the tastes of aesthetes the world over. Montesquiou in France, Count Primoli in Italy, the Grand Duke of Hesse-Darmstadt in Germany, along with countless amateurs, collected photographs, and took their own. An orgy of artistic ambition followed the arrival of dry-plate photography, where the effects of mystery sought by painters like Whistler or Carrière, as well as the elegant eroticism beloved of the period, seemed to be within the reach of anyone with the few pounds necessary to purchase equipment. Berlin was during the 1880s a modernist city, devoted to the high-minded aestheticism – in dress, architecture and the applied arts – which blossomed more rustically under the aegis of William Morris in England. With a national predisposition to science, the Germans were an ideal audience for photography. Alfred spent nine years of his life in a city where major government-sponsored exhibitions revealed the newest creations of the decade, fresh from palette, draughting-table or darkroom. This heady experience must have influenced the conviction and enthusiasm with which he presented the newest productions of our century to New Yorkers.

Returning to that city in 1890, he married, two years later, a quiet beautiful woman from his own background, Emmeline Obermeyer, and edited photographic journals: first the

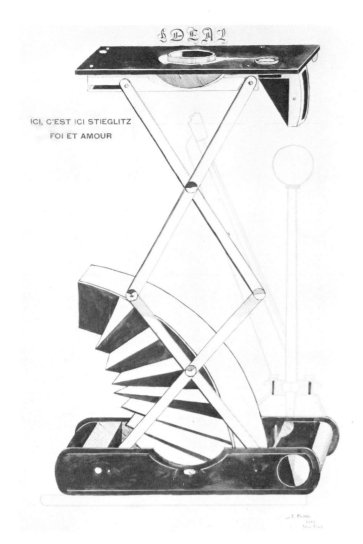

ICI, C'EST ICI STIEGLITZ
FOI ET AMOUR

72 (*Above*) *Distinguished Air* by Charles Demuth, 1930. Stieglitz showed this witty erotic watercolour suggesting a gutsy American response to Brancusi's *Mlle de Pogany*. (*14 × 12 ins. Coll. of Whitney Museum of American Art, Gift of the Friends*)

71 (*Above*) *Ici, c'est ici Stieglitz* by Francis Picabia, 1915. This artist's clever automotive-erotic images delighted Stieglitz, who became the loyal patron and impresario commemorated in this fantasia on the theme of *Camera Work*. (*Pen, red and black ink, 29⅞ × 20 ins. Metropolitan Museum of Art, Stieglitz Coll.*)

70 (*Left*) *New York Central Yards* by Stieglitz. Born in the United States of the 'Railway Baron' period, he recorded the raw scenes of his native land with the plate camera: his sensitivity to the mechanized society predisposed him to the modernist aesthetic

American Amateur Photographer, then *Camera Notes*, and finally the magazine identified with his name, *Camera Work*. He organized exhibitions of photographs, and took numerous subtle Whistlerian pictures of New York City, whose rising skyscrapers and smoggy avenues had not yet received such sensitive treatment. The squabbles and intimacies of the various camera clubs then extant in the metropolis occupied much of his time, introducing him not only to other cameramen, Gertrude Käsebier and F. Holland Day for example, but also to artists and collectors like Arthur Davies and John Quinn. In 1905 all this activity culminated in the foundation of the Photo-Secession Gallery, where up-to-date camera work and the newest creations of his artists were shown. The very name harks back to Germany, where, as in Vienna, the name *Sezessionstil* was associated with the last phases of German *art nouveau*, and where photography had received some of its earliest accolades. Aware, however, that this reference was already a dated one, Stieglitz, in 1908, changed the gallery name to *291* (the number of its Fifth Avenue address), and entered history.

291. A racy, modernist idea, to name a gallery after an address: impersonal, memorable, free from stylistic associations, the name suggested that gossip in Stieglitz's world reached beyond the novelties of photographic printing techniques, and caught *frissons* from the proto-Dadaist world in Paris. The numbers 291, like those Picasso and Braque incorporated into cubist paintings, were also chronometers of the future, suggesting the numbers Stieglitz's discovery Joseph Stella was later to elevate to the status of painterly subject-matter in themselves; they suggest the serial cognomens Brancusi applied to his 'Birds in Space' sculptures, I, II, III, and so forth, but also the businesslike names of New York's monoliths, often as anonymous as the numbered streets on which they were built. Most of all they were as apparently inappropriate a gallery logo as the name of an epoch-making exhibition which is intimately bound up with Stieglitz's position in the progression of American art: the Armory Show.

This extraordinary selection of European and American modern art, held at New York's

73 (*Left*) *Nude descending a staircase* by Marcel Duchamp, 1912. This canvas was the great *succès de scandale* of the Armory Show. (*58 × 35 ins. Philadelphia Museum of Art, Louise and Walter Arensberg Coll.*)

74 (*Below*) At the historic Armory Show, of which Stieglitz was a director, a small group of New York artists and collectors assembled an astonishing (if unbalanced) cross-section of European modern art. The result was a good-humoured free-for-all and a lasting US market for modernism

75 A self-avowed anchorite, Georgia O'Keeffe (here with Mrs Chester Dale) was nonetheless happy to abandon her New Mexico life on occasion, in favour of the highly remunerative exhibitions staged for her by Stieglitz

69th Regiment Armory, was in some respects heralded by Stieglitz's daring at *291*. It certainly left the gallery with a reputation of carrying the standard the show had run up. Before the Armory Show Stieglitz had mostly exhibited new photographic work by Alvin Langdon Colburn, Clarence White or the young Eduard Steichen; but he had also shown figure drawings by Rodin, woodcuts by Eric Gill, Japanese prints, Matisse watercolours and pictures by the American painter John Marin. What counted was the atmosphere in which these exhibitions were held. Without ornament of any kind, the severe rooms of his gallery invited excited conversation. Stieglitz was always there, ready to argue or discuss with all comers. In this heady air ideas from Paris, youthful impetuosities from local painters, and the opinions of older intellectuals cross-pollinated New York culture.

On the eve of World War One some of these artists decided to create a grand show of all the daring or venturesome things being done in the arts at the time. This was no band of Cocteau-like society aesthetes in silk cravats, nor of rowdy *Bateau-Lavoir* bohemians, but rather of serious tweed-clad Americans looking for fresh ideas and a good clearing of the air. America at the time idolized Sargent, and laughed at the not very daring works of Winslow Homer or Arthur Davies. London, however, had just been shocked by Roger Fry's Post-Impressionist Exhibition; something of this order was obviously necessary in the world's fastest-growing city. A selection committee made a whirlwind tour of Europe, gathering in Maillol, Picasso, the Duchamp brothers, and Matisse. American artists were selected; the

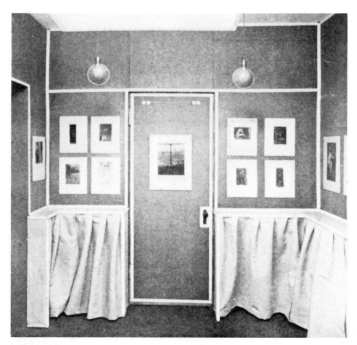

76 (*Left*) In the early years of the century Stieglitz exhibited and sold the works of his photographer friends, together with those of a few artists from both sides of the Atlantic, in his tiny plain gallery, Photo-Secession

77 (*Below*) In the Photo-Secession gallery, Elie Nadelman's sculpture stands out in clear relief against O'Keeffe's carefully mixed grey tones. This gallery's trend-setting move rendered art photogenic, something the art world has found indispensable ever since

78 Tireless enthusiast and dapper charmer, Stieglitz sold
modern art by talking about it. The ladies' groups, wealthy
housewives and teachers who still support modern art in
America were his audience. Here he examines one of O'Keeffe's
austere images, *The Bone*

79 At *291*, his renamed gallery, Stieglitz expanded his stock to include African fetishes (under the influence of Picasso) and Brancusi sculpture

Armory rented; and, when the doors opened on such exhibits as Marcel Duchamp's *Nude Descending a Staircase*, a storm of laughter and applause hit the show like a tidal wave. In the long run, the Armory Show, with Stieglitz on the Board of Directors, *did* open the eyes of the United States to modern art, starting a trend for adventurous collecting and spirited public discussion which has endured to this day. After its official closure, Stieglitz carried on exhibiting the foreign artists who had sent work to the Armory Show, as well as forming close personal friendships and professional ties with the American painters who had also made their mark. Indeed, as the 1920s progressed, he concentrated on the Americans, deciding, as was particularly true of Georgia O'Keeffe, that there was a strong vein of non-derivative native modernism which needed developing.

The man who did all this was remarkable, obviously. That he was also charming, forthright, quietly handsome (Stieglitz dressed the part of a businessman, in steel-rimmed glasses, discreet bow-ties, tweeds, and the occasional Inverness cape or long overcoat), was an advantage which endeared him to all the visitors to his gallery. In 1924 he married O'Keeffe, whom he had made a rich woman through judicious sales of her canvases, and moved with her to various hotel apartments. They were early seekers after a serviceable asceticism which remains at a premium in New York. The taste of his hard-eyed, straight-backed wife influenced his own, and led to the plain white walls and unpretentious exhibitions held at his

80 *Razor* by Gerald Murphy, 1924. Through Stieglitz's encouragement artists as unlikely as Scott Fitzgerald's friend Murphy created images both original and cosmopolitan. This canvas predates Pop Art by 50 years and results from an association with Fernand Léger. (*32 × 36 ins. Dallas Museum of Art, Gift of Artist*)

new galleries, The Intimate Gallery and An American Place. O'Keeffe spent part of each year in the windswept Southwest she explored in her paintings; Navajo artefacts, desert rocks, plain wood furniture and practical clothes were new, Shaker-like austerities she made, if not fashionable, recognizable as an eclectic taste which has supplied a hallmark for generations of American bohemians, and has recently become a consciously nationalistic style in interior decoration.

Perhaps the home-grown artists Stieglitz exhibited were not among the greatest (Charles Demuth was witty, Marsden Hartley serious but maladroit, O'Keeffe herself limited by intellectual isolation); perhaps the Europeans he showed were already established in the firmament of Modernism (Picasso, Picabia, Duchamp and Brancusi did, however, profit directly and indirectly from the immense American market he opened for their work); his own photography was perhaps a more lasting and beautiful achievement than his promotional enterprise. But as a type, the cultured first-generation American, who responded to what Ian Dunlop has flawlessly called 'The Shock of the New', Stieglitz set a tone for numerous Americans since his time. The marriage of art and commerce, which has its ramifications in the lives of later arbiters, was in Stieglitz's case perfectly clothed in a hearty, benevolent manner, a Calvinist sobriety and an insistence on work of value which suited the raw but willing first generation of modernist collectors in the United States. His friends,

81 (*Left*) Photograph of George Tooker by Paul Cadmus, c. 1948. Cadmus's neo-classical tempera pictures often suggest the satirical exoticism of Demuth

82 (*Below*) Philip Johnson's Glass House at New Canaan, Connecticut: an example of the aesthetic inheritance of Stieglitz's new American style

83 (*Right*) A real 'American Place' was finally found for US modernism in 1939, when New York's Museum of Modern Art was built. Stieglitz was on the first board of directors

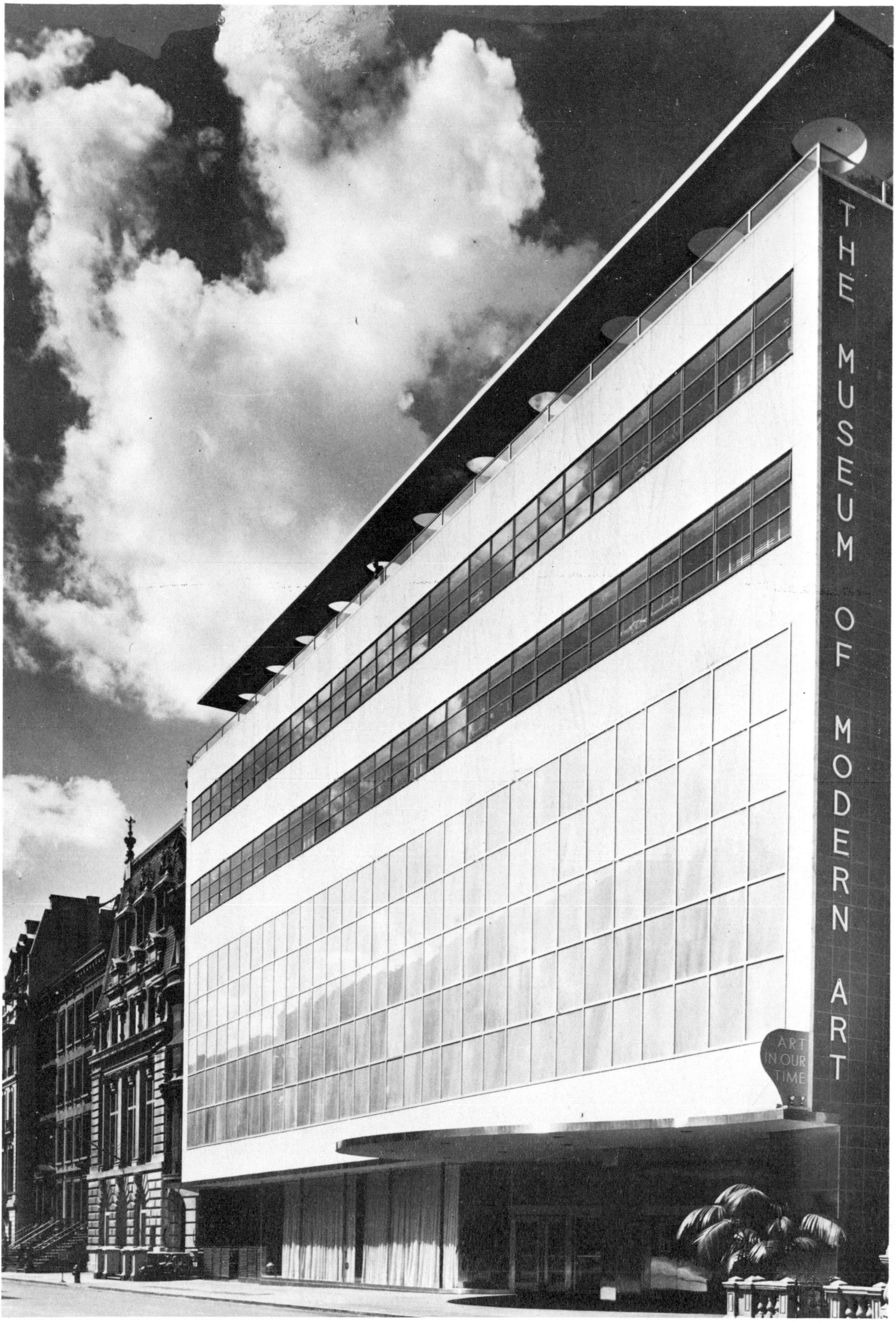
THE MUSEUM OF MODERN ART
ART IN OUR TIME

84 Georgia O'Keeffe (here with her painting *Life and Death*, 1931), as beautiful an object in her home-made nun-like habits as she was a rare spirit, became Stieglitz's great contribution to American aesthetics

Eugene Meyer and his extraordinary wife (who paid the duty on Brancusi's submissions to the Armory Show, getting them past resistant customs officials as bathroom fittings), Monroe Wheeler, first head of New York's Museum of Modern Art, or Solomon Guggenheim, founder of the museum which bears his name, all looked up to or benefited from Stieglitz's opinionated but benign presence as a *paterfamilias* to the art world. The almost Japanese, but at the same time proudly puritan restraint of his polemic for the new art recurs constantly as a

85 A pueblo of the Taos Indians, New Mexico, where Georgia O'Keeffe spent much time and gained inspiration. The pueblo and the glass box (Plate 82) have remained the Janus-faces of US intellectuals

theme in avant-garde circles all over the world; it is perfectly summed up in the words of a printed card he posted on the grey hessian walls of An American Place:

> *NO* formal Press views
> *NO* cocktail parties
> *NO* special invitations
> *NO* advertising
> *NO* institution
> *NO* isms
> *NO* theories
> *NO* game being played
> *Nothing* asked of anyone who comes
> *NO* anything on the walls except *what you see there*
> *The doors of An American Place are ever open to all.*

86 Marinetti in his role as champion of the Futurists. The military moustache and dandy's gloves belie the poet

Filippo Marinetti
1876–1944

F. T. Marinetti

During the same years when Robert de Montesquiou instructed the Parisian *gratin* in the nuances of aesthetics, when Diaghilev solicited funds for his barbaric invasion, and Lady Mendl made her first tentative steps as combined social figure and professional decorator, a breath of artistic revolution blew north across the Alps from Italy. Though in part a fusion of the Cubist ideas fostered in Picasso's younger, poorer days with the egocentric Don Juanism of Italy's own brand of *fin-de-siècle* decadence, the movement launched by Filippo Marinetti was a masculine, aggressive novelty. 'Futurism', he called his wave of contrary thought; despite this ringing appellation, he first preached sweeping artistic change to the same *saloneurs* who applauded Diaghilev, and only later to the workers and bourgeoisie who became his strongest supporters. In the elegance of the movement, in its use of poetry and publicity, and in its very dilettantism lay the seeds of its curious flowering, not as a constantly-changing revolutionary philosophy, which it first appeared to be, but as something that became an altogether more inflexible monolith not only in the history of style but elsewhere: Fascism.

It is difficult today to link the shattered images on canvas, maniacal displays of accidental music or word collages, and hysterical public behaviour which spring to mind when we hear the word 'Futurism' with the chill neo-classicism, impersonal efficiency and historicist grandiloquence associated with Fascism. Both -isms were, however, preoccupied with the Nietzschean myth of the hero, and sought to reach towards a new world – no one ever claimed that that new world would be cast in a democratic mould. Indeed, in a still royal Europe it was hardly expected to be. An aesthetic revolution in the Italy of Umberto I was, thanks to the nature of patronage and cultism, essentially a palace revolution, but the absorption of the Futurist outlook into the Fascist outrage does mark a unique twentieth-century example of taste as a widespread political weapon. If the characters of the polemicist politician Danton and the propagandist painter David had been fused, the result might have resembled Filippo Marinetti.

His parents were the first moneyed members of a lower-middle-class Milanese family, enriched by his father's stock-market speculations. Contemporary of Diaghilev, Beardsley and Stieglitz, Marinetti grew up with a generation that was the last to believe in continuing world peace and a status quo in society. This cultured generation, by 1900, was stifling in the static, hot-house atmosphere perpetuated by the intellectuals of the 1890s. A pre-eminently Italian desire for glory and heroic action was in the air, disseminated by the novelist Gabriele d'Annunzio's inferior poems, exemplified by inspiring national spectacles like the composer Giuseppe Verdi's grandiloquent funeral in 1901. Marinetti had benefited from the commercial modernity of Milan and his mother's determination to see her son proficient in the arts. With a generalized interest in poetry, painting and literature, he was by 1908 aware of the unique position waiting for a new occupant in the whirlpool of Italian taste. The great national poets were either dead (Carducci, in 1907, died a Senator and public oracle of morality) or exiled (d'Annunzio, the national Byron, fled debts and irate mistresses to live in

Paris until 1919). Their places had been enviable, combining political power with artistic idolatry. Already a prize-winning poet, rich, versatile and bursting with ideas, Marinetti knew there was an opportunity to seize, and, announcing himself as 'the caffeine of Europe', he set about doing so in a lively and amusing way. He became a sort of human newspaper, reporting all the developments in modern art that came to his notice, with intensive editorial comment designed to promote a loosely-formulated philosophy of change and struggle in society through art. This was a step beyond Diaghilev, whose ambitions were purely artistic. The motives of both were, however, comparable, based in an affluent childhood, an indifferent parent, and an erotic impulse.

Marinetti *père* had made his fortune in Egypt. In Alexandria Filippo's older brother had died, leaving the younger son to take up the role of poet and intellectual which had been reserved for the first-born. In the Egypt of the Khedives the young man had witnessed marvels as old as time, and the modern phenomenon of commerce surrounding the Suez Canal: a fusion of these things with his father's pronounced taste for erotica mixed with religion (tracts on both subjects were read to the older man by hired prostitutes) lies at the root of Filippo's curious intellectual jargon. The stridency with which he promoted his ideas follows the poetic actions of Italian heroes, Carducci, Garibaldi, or the Principessa Bel-

87 Futurist drawings contrast oddly with the décor of his father's bourgeois flat, from which Marinetti carried on his campaign for a new artistic and social order. Here he poses (centre, seated) with (l. to r.) Cinti, Russolo, Mazza, Buzzi and Boccioni

88 *Unique Forms of Continuity in Space* by Umberto Boccioni, 1913. Boccioni's is the figurehead image of high Futurism. (*Bronze, cast 1931; 43⅞ × 34⅞ × 15¾ ins. Museum of Modern Art, New York, Lillie P. Bliss Bequest*)

89 Like Marinetti, Mussolini came from a world that craved the stolid masculine traditionalism we can see in this photograph of his study in the Villa Torlonia

giojoso, who had contributed a theatricality to the mid-nineteenth-century Risorgimento movement for the unification of Italy. It was in this tradition that Marinetti, at twenty-four, toured Italy and France as a declaimer of verse, reading his poems from suburban stages to audiences combining the aesthetes and the workers. His reading of the Futurist Manifesto from the campanile in Venice, preceded by trumpet blasts and a shower of crimson leaflets, was merely an Americanized application of this pre-TV form of entertainment; the manner had more to it than the message.

Throughout the war years and the 1920s, Marinetti was ubiquitous in Europe. His large private fortune capitalized exhibitions of painting (by Severini, Boccioni or Balla, who, stimulated by advances in physics, all attempted to paint sequential movement), concerts (by Russolo or Pratella, who experimented with irrational and *concrète* music), and demonstrations (the shouting, insults and leaflet-throwing in Futurist Soirées have become legendary). He took his band of associates throughout Italy, to Germany, and to France. He solicited the participation of foreign artists in the movement, roping in talents as disparate as those of the French poet Guillaume Apollinaire, the Russian painters Natalia Gontcharova and Mikhail Larionov, the English painter and writer Wyndham Lewis, and even the American poet Hart Crane. He assimilated Cubist theory and Parisian bohemianism into his attitude, a robust traditional machismo which also encompassed a veneration of war veterans and an aesthetic of violence devoted to memories of wartime male bonding and heroic

90 'The Caffeine of Europe', Marinetti poses with the panache
of a modern Don Juan in one of the cafés where modern art was
processed

91 (*Left*) *La Duchesse de la Salle* by T. de Lempicka, 1925: a French equivalent of that glacially pseudo-modernist art adopted by conservative people who felt the need to fuse the avant-garde and tradition. (*Galerie Alain Blondel, Paris*)

92 D'Annunzio, role-model for Marinetti, could admire a battleship, the Puglia, planted in his garden at Gardone in commemoration of his conquest at Fiume. The gesture and the gesticulation predicted Futurist excesses

93 (*Left*) Mussolini addressing the crowd in Rome. Tawdry would-be Imperial panoply surrounded his official life

94 (*Below*) The Roman pomp of Fascism was never far from the theatrical megalomania evident in such productions as the 1930s film *Ben-Hur* – shot in Rome

95 Response to Fascism was confused at first.
It is hard to say if this *coiffeur*'s window
display was produced in irony or naive
patriotism

sacrifice. In this trend-setting amalgam of unlikely opposites, Marinetti produced the climate
for Fascism. The style itself he only partly inspired; Mussolini's neo-classical follies were
themselves hybrids of Futurist sleekness and d'Annunzian historicism. Visually speaking,
the Fascist style combines the gilt bronze muscles of Boccioni's *Unique Forms of Continuity in
Space* (1913) and the plaster casts of Michelangelo's 'Slaves' in d'Annunzio's villa Guar-
dareale. While the latter is retrograde and meretricious, we must understand that, through
the agency of Mussolini, the contemporary public saw it endowed with the modernist
glamour of the former. If this seems laughable today, it is vital to understand that our derision
is different from the fascinated opposition with which Marinetti's farrago of ideas was
greeted by his own public.

The apartment left him by his father, in which Marinetti spent most of his domestic life,
was not the temple of modernity one might have expected. Appallingly Egyptianized, it
boasted a Victorian clutter of bazaar brassworks, dusty carpets and dark wood relieved here
and there by a Coptic mummy-case portrait or dubious faiences. This eclectic mess was,
however, linked to the creations of Bugatti, whose astrological chambers, lined in parchment,
combined materials with true nineteenth-century whimsy, and who based furniture shapes

96   From the modernism of Futurist
sculpture, Fascist official art retained an aura
of modernity and caricatured masculinity,
here used to decorate the Mussolini forum in
Rome

98 (*Right*) Again the aesthetic of repeated forms
and the literalness of Futurism contribute to a
Fascist monument, in this case an *art concret*
representation of the soldiers' roll-call in a war
monument for the dead of the African campaign

97 (*Right*) The partial
frivolity of Fascist style
assumed an altogether less
graceful stance in the
hands of Adolf Hitler,
who borrowed it for his
own poetry of machines,
to terrible effect

more on architectural reveries than considerations of comfort. The Futurists were, on the whole, too busy demonstrating, or too poor, to create décors – but the rushing images of their paintings, and the smashed instruments or torn-up reproductions viewed at their happenings, were sources for the Dada interiors (like Kurt Schwitters' famous Merzbau in Hamburg) which led in turn to Surrealist conglomerates of objects and furniture. It is the work of Marinetti's sculptor friends, more academic but more striking than that of the painters, which is seminal for Fascism. The Italian taste for monumental, exaggeratedly figurative pieces of architecture and sculpture combined in these works to produce strange hard-edged images such as Boccioni's *Head + House + Light* (1912), which actually includes a human bust, a window frame and solidified rays of light. The appearance of this kind of work, usually exhibited in plaster, was white, square, muscular, and actually suggests a sort of automotive neo-classicism rather than the Picassoesque novelty it was intended to have. Minus the aesthetic/scientific bias, plus the political propagandism Mussolini required, the taste for Futurist sculpture obviously predisposed the thinking public to the slightly ludicrous mundane heroism represented by the Milan railway station or the athletes surrounding the *Stado Mussolini* in Rome.

99 A historical pageant (the inauguration of a *casa del fascio*) in Tuscany suggests the strain of play-acting in Fascism, and a view of d'Annunzian grandiloquence to which Marinetti, surprisingly, responded

101 (*Right*) Florence station, even more than the glories of Milan, reveals the influence of Futurist streamlining and its adulation of speed on Fascist ambitions

100 (*Right*) Grandiose neo-classicism also made its appearance in Paris: this electric train and its background of the Palais de Chaillot at the 1937 exhibition express the fusion of two Futurist themes

102 Felice Casorati, *Double portrait*, 1924. Even
in private portraiture, the Futurist ideals of
nobility of gesture, merged with an elegant but
retardataire classicism, produced a short-lived
Fascist style

103 (*Above*) A view of the Mussolini forum, a sports stadium designed to give the people bread and circuses in the Roman manner. The 'circuses' were the soccer or gymnastics the Futurists had painted and praised

104 (*Right*) King Vittorio Emanuele III, Marinetti and Mussolini personify Tradition, Futurism, and Fascism at the 1933 Exhibition of Futurist Art in Rome

PAROLE CONSONANTI VOCALI NUMERI **IN LIBERTÀ**

Dal volume, di prossima pubblicazione: **"I PAROLIBERI FUTURISTI „:**
(AURO D'ALBA, BALLA, BETUDA, BOCCIONI, BUZZI, CAMPIGLI, CANGIULLO, CARRÀ, CAVALLI, BRUNO CORRA, D. CORRENTI, M. DEL GUERRA, DELLA FLORESTA, L. FOLGORE, A. FRANCHI, C. GOVONI. GUIZZIDORO, ITTAR, JANNELLI, MARINETTI, ARMANDO MAZZA, PRESENZINI-MATTOLI, RADIANTE, SETTIMELLI, TODINI, ecc.)

MARINETTI, *parolibero*. — Montagne + Vallate + Strade × Joffre

Somewhat surprisingly, Marinetti responded to the new order when it came in 1922. In this context we must recollect that Futurism depended on journalism for the publication of its ideas. In 1919 an anti-Left demonstration in Milan attracted the participation of the Futurists; they were present at the organization of the bullying cohorts who quashed Bolshevist demonstrators. These councils took place at the offices of Mussolini's newspaper, the *Popolo d'Italia*, and culminated in the burning, by Futurist youths, of his old paper, now a Communist organ, *Avanti!* Is this style, we may ask, is it Art? For the turbulent post-war European intellectuals who wanted to relate aesthetics to changes in morality, it was. No one was more adept at the irresponsible juggling required for this marriage of introspection and action than Marinetti; that is precisely why Mussolini, at this stage, cultivated him. When the Fascists had achieved power, Marinetti was to see himself supplanted by the ageing d'Annunzio, who returned to Italy, his debts paid by the government, to preside as a spurred and booted Merlin to the lavatory-marble Camelot of the *Duce*.

Marinetti and his docile wife moved to Rome, where the shining monuments of the new efficiency were freezing the constantly mobile future he had imagined. His dreams of speed and dynamism in modern life seemed to boil down to the functional train schedule for which Mussolini has remained famous. The anti-aristocrat and professional blasphemer supported the king and praised the church. This was not a contradictory hypocrisy; rather, it was another step in the fundamentally confused vogueishness of Futurism. It was not really such a tremendous step from writing, in the first Futurist Manifesto (1913):

105 (*Above left*) This revolving head of Mussolini by P. Bertelli in the Imperial War Museum, London, combines a Fascist classical aesthetic with the dynamic movement in space explored by Marinetti's artists. The sense of madness suits the subject

106 (*Above right*) The witty hysteria of Futurist graphics (here dealing with poetry and music in a jumbled style that predates Punk by 70 years) reads retrospectively like a cartoon voice-over for speeches by Mussolini or Hitler

They'll see us crouched beside our trembling airplanes in the act of warming our hands at the poor little blaze that our books of today will give out when they take fire from the flight of our images

to rhapsodizing the violent generation in a late poem,

The voluptuous first line of battle vibrates like long stretched cords strummed by projectiles ... We will be we are the kneeling machine-guns whose barrels throb with prayer...

Nor was the revenge on polite society, implicit in association with the Napoleonic usurper Mussolini, an alien pleasure to the man who had proved himself so accomplished a hater in speeches called 'We abjure our Symbolist Masters', or 'Against Past-Loving Venice'. The tragedy is that visual as well as moral goodness was lost in the tumult of verbiage which Marinetti bequeathed to Fascism. *Arma virumque cano* was the poetry of the *Duce*'s regime; it had been the subterranean refrain of Futurism, but art and elegance had diluted it. The humanism of Cubism or Russian Constructivism is evident in the political opposition to the Right maintained by Picasso in France, or Tatlin and Malevitch in Russia. Stirring the same cauldron of thought, Futurism veered towards a racist, imperialist, right-wing insanity for sadly theatrical reasons, in pursuit of that artistic machismo and nationalist glamour which are perhaps inescapable in Italian aesthetics.

In so doing, the movement spawned a short-lived style of official architecture, sculpture and painting which, despite its associations, has been confounded with Corbusier-based functionalism, and lingers in the chill expanse of official government art the world over. The fusion of opposites this represents is crystallized in the head of Mussolini, labelled 'DUX' (or 'Leader') in Roman letters, by Bertelli: the revolving profile, a Futurist concept of an object in many locations simultaneously, becomes a phallic finial of pseudo-Roman grandeur, its movement confined to one plinth, and thus suggesting the frenzied spinning of a madman. The madness was, however, a popular one – it is the insanity which defended Ezra Pound from charges of betraying his country, the paranoia of Wyndham Lewis against the art establishment in England, and the monomania preserved in d'Annunzio's home. It was Futurism, a looking forward which failed to take account of the present, a refashioning of style based on the destruction of style itself.

107 Surrounded with
portraits by Christian
Bérard and Sir Francis
Rose, Cecil Beaton
telephones at a table by
Giacometti in a classic
pose reminiscent of
fashion-world gossip

Sir Cecil Beaton
1904–1980

Just a little younger than our century, Cecil Beaton was always just a bit ahead of current taste, his image never avant-garde, but always reassuringly near the height of British fashion. His parents were examples of the genteel moderately affluent middle-class society whose lifestyle, to the Edwardians, seemed immutable. In his published diaries and memoirs Beaton records a fierce determination to break out of the stifling cocoon their love and incomprehension wove around him. With this ambition, however, he combined an increasing nostalgia for the ease and grace of a vanishing epoch witnessed from a child's eyes. The fusion of such opposing attitudes determined a hybrid personality, dedicated to the new and surprising in all the arts, but waspish, critical and snobbish in loyalty to established institutions.

Feeling keenly he had somewhere other than his natural habitat to attain, Beaton kept his emotions to himself (and his diary), silently filing away every new experience – every flower, face and fashion – to form a vast armoury for visual composition. This composition, he hoped from schooldays on, would be in the line of theatrical design. Instead it erupted, after a false start in his father's timber-broking business, into a vein of real novelty in photography. Armed with his nanny's pocket Kodak, Beaton improvised images of his Oxford and Cambridge friends, which, in retrospect, were often clumsy amateur pastiches of work by the great Edwardian cameramen Baron de Meyer or E. O. Hoppé. But to his contemporaries these repainted negatives yielded a form of cheerful flattery which suited the needs of the time, and led, as if by accident, to a lifelong career, an international reputation and a knighthood.

Cecil Beaton went to school with Evelyn Waugh, who bullied him; like two sides of a coin, Waugh and Beaton were later to emerge as types of 1920s snobbery, both achieving success by creative work, both becoming rich, both investing the English class structure with a romantic glamour it was fast losing after World War One. Each developed a conspicuous and stylized manner of speech, each was notable for individual habits of dress, each relied on forms of wit and panache for their social conquests. It is fitting that they cordially loathed each other.

Harrow widened the circle of Beaton's acquaintance, developing his interest in theatre and the arts (he made several appearances as a woman in school plays), and served as a preamble to his years at Cambridge. The events of those college years suggest the personal characteristics Beaton had to overcome in his self-promotion. Though he went up to Cambridge during the 1920s, his effeminacy, hissing speech and slightly over-refined aestheticism were too much for his peers; humiliatingly dumped in the river during a ball at Wilton House, Beaton was obliged to toughen himself in preparation for his attack on *le beau monde*. He was offensive to English society of the times not because he was homosexual (England being a country where such figures as Beau Brummell are firmly established in the communal memory), nor because he was keen on the arts (this was more dangerous in a decade when hunting and fishing and tweeds were still very much the attributes of a gentleman) – but

108 As a young man Beaton's taste absorbed from the sophisticated world a baroque extravagance which he deployed at a small country house called Ashcombe

109 Going further than
his masters, Beaton
created lavish décors for
his personal life out of
flea-market bits and
pieces. His friends joined
the masquerade
throughout the 1920s

110 Designed by Rex
Whistler, executed by
circus merry-go-round
manufacturers, Beaton's
bed exemplified his own
tinsel pastiche of the
grander decorative trends
of his times

111 The pink and white
femininity of Lady
Anglesey's bedroom at
Plas Newydd seems
commonplace today. In
the Twenties it
represented that up-to-
date luxury and conscious
'decoration' which pleased
Beaton and his circle, and
greatly contrasted with
dark stodgy inherited
interiors

because he belonged to that social entity then as now slightly risible to rulers and workers alike, the Middle Classes. The world of *Howard's End*, the novel in which E. M. Forster lovingly but scathingly criticized this genteel milieu, was a far cry from that of Diaghilev or the musical stage, to which magazines and daydreams had led the young Beaton in his imagination. Nevertheless, the little Kodak, and Cecil's impromptu settings, whipped up from silver foil, household bric-à-brac and costume boxes, somehow managed to suggest just the theatricality he longed for. In every proper Englishman hides a serious desire to misbehave, to dress up, to be chic; by fulfilling these wishes in his faintly ridiculous personal appearance, Beaton protected the pleasure his work provided: the mockery became accept- able flattery. His first exhibition of photographs and drawings did very well, launching him into a world where his social acumen could yield handsome profits.

Yield them it did. By the time he was thirty Beaton, like Lady Mendl (who abetted his first steps in the fashion world), had created a fees scale which fed on the snobbishness of his work; when Condé Nast in New York gave him an exclusive contract to write, draw and photograph for *Vogue* he must have begun to lose the envy his diary records for decorators and artists more successful than himself. But more than that, he joined a family, the fashion world, which cocooned his professional life in a communal hustle-and-bustle very like Diaghilev's busy circus. His friends at home and abroad also formed interlocking coteries, which gave him, and his work, that feeling of being 'on the inside' so important to his worldly success. That Beaton's place in these coteries was professional as much as personal was a sign of the

times, like the emergence of the decorator as arbiter of taste, and marks the arrival of the photographer as a power in the history of ideas. The mix of professionals and aristocrats, citizens of different countries and all levels of intellect in these coteries marks a change in the purpose of taste itself; for the Twenties and Thirties taste was not an aesthetic, a reflection of politics or a private pleasure – it was *fun*.

The tradition of Diaghilev provided an example of fashion originating with spectacle; Beaton seized the need for a private counterpart to this, providing, at his photographic sittings, or in his own entertainments, an amateur charade which gave his clients, employers and friends the sense of escape they had previously only felt at performances of *Schéhérazade* or *Petroushka*. This amusement coincided with the development of the snapshot camera, which itself added to social life an element of voyeuristic fun which is still with us. The word 'amateur' is a salient one in Beaton's career; in matters of taste and art the English, whose historical roles have always been by preference vainglorious, have no place for the artist by profession; the *dilettante* or *amateur des arts* has a better chance of acceptance in a society which fears the unfamiliar. Beaton's lack of technical training, his improvisatory talent, and the air of party-time he brought to his work all tallied with the tastes of his sitters; in applauding him, they applauded themselves. Beaton, however, was a shrewd man who recognized these issues, used them, and held on firmly to every inch of status he was given. In this aspect he was very English; his un-English aesthetic enthusiasms qualify him as a taste-

112 (*Above*) Beaton's personal never-never land was given substance of a sort by the exquisite *trompe l'oeil* fantasies of Rex Whistler, whose dining-room at Plas Newydd featured a quasi-Italian scene suffused with sunlight and lavish decorative elements

113 (*Right*) Rex Whistler working on the mural at Plas Newydd with Diana Cooper's sister and her husband, the Marquess of Anglesey. Rex's fluent talent and fey charm made him a figure to envy for the more waspish, less specifically talented Beaton

114 Charles James' Bernini-esque satin dresses answered
Beaton's longings for luxury and genius in the minor arts.
He paid tribute to the 'Leonardo of Couture' in this inspired
photograph

115 (*Right*) Beaton's drawings were excellent when based on
photographs. This wash and line portrait of his beloved friend
and envied fellow arbiter Peter Watson shows the influence of
Bérard on his style, and of the 1920s ideal male on his
emotional outlook

116 Snapping his own portrait in Christian Bérard's squalid
Paris hotel room, Beaton participated in the worldly,
improvisatory Bohemia he himself represented to middle–class
England

maker in a country where such figures have usually been women or aristocrats.

In this context it is valuable to know that Cecil Beaton more or less grew up along with fashion magazines. As such, they had not existed much before the *Gazette du Bon Ton*, in 1904, commissioned photographers to make records of couture dresses, and began to publish articles about these clothes, and the jewels, hats, shoes and social life which went along with them. Before this magazines, even when they dealt with fashion and the arts, were primarily concerned with the comings and goings of that upper class who wore the dresses and bought the pictures. England's *Tatler* continued in this vein for many years; but the American publisher Condé Nast's *Vogue*, in New York and London, subtly altered its coverage to the things themselves. Snobbish in the extreme, *Vogue*, and later *Harper's*, its rival, nonetheless used an effective psychological blackmail in its promotion: it explained fashion, beauty treatments, social niceties, etc, in a way which pleased if you were already proficient at them, and goaded to achievement if you were not. In doing this it created, by the time Beaton began to work in journalism, an effective platform for taste-making which, though commercial, began to acquire all the status of an institution. Here the matrix of style became public, dictated to a certain extent by the commercial interest of designers and manufacturers; the intelligent interpretation through stylish writing, drawing and photography, which Beaton supplied, was thus essentially advertisement, not for his own tastes, but for trends which had degenerated into produce. Thus the role of the arbiter acquired a tinge of hypocrisy, being to a certain extent the outcome of a successful collaboration with business interests and a bogus canonization by the media. Where the aristocrats had followed personal whims, creating new genres of Edwardian taste, and the decorators had elevated their own business into taste-making, Beaton, by the late Twenties, was in the vanguard of figures whose work for other people appeared to be personal selectivity but was actually a wide-scale commercialization of the role of *arbiter elegantiarum*, a parallel of the development of stage actors into movie stars.

Beaton satisfied his desire to succeed in one field by transferring its behaviour patterns to another. As arbiter extraordinaire he behaved with the flair and panache he had admired in musical stars, and found again in Broadway or Hollywood acquaintances. His wide-brimmed hats, flowing cravats, and natty suits all supported a witty new persona which the world at large, always in need of court entertainers, accepted as a new archetype. His education, increased income and personal charm guaranteed that, during the 1930s, Beaton was able to turn this novel character into an ubiquitous one, equally at home in the worlds of stage, screen and fashion magazine. That the trick was rather like his mannerist borrowings from painters for the décor of his photographs passed unnoticed, perhaps because of an acceptance of cross-pollination in the arts left behind by Diaghilev's experiment, and reinvigorated by the exhibitionistic surprises of the Surrealist movement – itself closely allied to fashion. Beaton's own taste was, for many years, a kind of loosely-derived drawing-room Surrealism, which preferred the nostalgic decorative whimsy of the movement to its Freudian probings.

In the decoration of Ashcombe, the small Georgian farmhouse in Wiltshire Beaton leased in 1930, there is nothing genuinely original, but nothing quite like accepted styles of the times. His bed, designed by Rex Whistler and made by a company which carved and gilded circus accoutrements, is exuberantly neo-Baroque, while the circus theme, which was carried on through murals, curtains, and furniture such as white-painted drums used as end-tables, refers loosely to Picasso's circus period. The bits of pseudo- (and real) rococo furniture in his drawing-room, the satin draperies, glittering bits of mirror, and extensive use of all-white schemes unite the wistful neo-Romantic taste launched in the mid-Twenties by Christian

117 While French Bohemianism led to the Louvre, its English
counterpart led to Buckingham Palace. The apex of Beaton's
career as a 'daring' photographer was the series of King George
VI and Queen Elizabeth which he took early in their reign

118 In later life Beaton reverted to the Edwardian styles of his childhood – following *and* leading public taste in the collecting of *art nouveau*, orchids and extravagant hats

119 (*Left*) Fonteyn and Nureyev in *Marguerite and Armand*. His own brand of modernism never far from nostalgia, Beaton became a pundit of the past, called upon to evoke romantic images for such creations as Frederick Ashton's 'Camille' ballet

120 (*Above*) Beaton remembered Bérard's sets for ballets like *Symphonie Pastorale* when he created his spare, chiffon-filled ballroom design for *Marguerite and Armand*

Bérard and Eugène Berman, young French painters, with the trendy bleached schemes of Syrie Maugham. Arms protruding from the walls as lamps, false ermine bed-curtains, fragments of statues and the whole temporariness of the décor all coincide with the pseudo-royal insignia, *trompe l'oeil*, and stagey grandeur introduced by Salvador Dali and the more decorative Surrealists such as Dominguez, Seligmann and Bellmer.

In this jumbled, witty and, most importantly, *impromptu* setting, Beaton acted out effete fantasies: *fêtes galantes*, period plays, Cocteau-ish movie-making. All these efforts, for which he used his friends, mostly drawn from the combined worlds of fashion and the intelligent aristocracy, were practice for the set designs and movie designs he provided during the 1940s and 1950s. Without Ashcombe (later supplanted by a more sedate paraphrase of the country seat, Reddish House, where he died), Beaton could never have achieved the credibility which led to postwar commissions for *Lady Windermere's Fan* (in which he also acted) or *School for Scandal* and the tremendous success of *My Fair Lady*. By the time he designed this last film, Beaton's taste, in tune with advancing age, a reputation as Photographer Royal (he 'did' the Coronation in 1953), and changes in established collections, had turned back to the *art nouveau* and historicist Edwardian objects of his youth. Using these things, and the ancient

121 (*Left*) By the time of his giant retrospective exhibition in London and New York (1968), Beaton had undergone a revival. His memories of the Twenties suited the extravagances of the swinging Sixties, when he was taken up by young photographers and artists (this photo is by Patrick Lichfield)

122 Childhood dreams of designing for the stage came true in the 1940s when Beaton was asked to evoke the turn of the century for Oscar Wilde's *Lady Windermere's Fan*. This backward-looking glamour reached his widest public yet

123 Willingness to admire
the young not surprisingly
endeared Beaton to the
youth of the Sixties. His
love of *art nouveau* and
enthusiasms for new
fashions (here modelled in
his bedroom by Twiggy)
were contemporary and
kept him in the forefront
of changing tastes

124 From Wilde to Shaw, Beaton fixed an image of the 1890s for the theatre-going public. Following on from the stage production, his designs for the film of *My Fair Lady* made his name a necessity on any period production and a world-wide synonym for opulence

English preoccupation with the garden which he developed at Reddish, Beaton achieved a perfect camp equivalent of the English Gentleman, successful enough to conceal any moral obstacles in the way of his knighthood.

The later, grander days of Beaton's life are always up-to-date, but less influential in the history of taste than his younger, flightier period. From 1925 to the Second World War he tactfully and charmingly introduced to England and America a pastel version of the perverse eclectic taste which fecundated Surrealism in France. Using a colour sense, an eye for furniture and his flair for presenting fantasies which derived from painterly or couture sources, Beaton bolstered the new insistence on amusement, shock and innovation as essentials to fashion. He concurrently left a flashlit record, in words and pictures, of many decades of people and things conforming to this demand. His compulsive work habits and discerning eye speeded up the process of trend-setting, aided by the monthly dissemination, in fashion magazines, of his *aperçus*. That the neo-Baroque taste itself was shoddy and ephemeral (the paintings of Christian Bérard being about its only surviving monuments of quality) is neither here nor there; that Beaton, creating and imitating this taste, helped create the Mode in the sense we think of it today is a distinguished personal effect to have had.

Vicomtesse
Marie-Laure de Noailles
1903–1970

Marie Laure

In 1934 the poet and artist Jean Cocteau wrote of

A very high wave which would sweep us ahead, pell-mell, tragically and joyously, with the films of Marlene Dietrich, extravagant fashions, plays which we took turns reading to one another, and the thousand and one spells cast by the Rue Vignon, where my room became the clasp of an extraordinary necklace of wave transmissions. Our gang wasn't really one. It grew more numerous by a gyratory phenomenon of molecular affinities, a kind of internal style. But it remained inaccessible to those who pulled strings in order to become part of it.

Wealth, a taste for luxury, literature, art, drugs, and, most of all, the concept and practice of 'Modernism' bound this gang that was not a gang, forming a hybrid style resembling the accidental juxtapositions of a junk-shop. Founder-member of the group, teenage friend of Cocteau, and idiosyncratic muse of Paris before the Second World War was Marie-Laure de Noailles. In order to understand the often invisible qualities which were her credentials as an arbiter of style in Cocteau's Parisian circus, it is necessary to understand the priorities of her friends, and their derivation.

Cocteau had won his social spurs, and some artistic *réclame*, in the wake of Diaghilev's Russian Ballet. A handsome young poet, he attached himself to the troupe of dancers, entertaining them, drawing them, and finally providing them with the scenario of his ill-fated *Dieu Bleu*. In exchange, the Russians provided this essentially middle-class charmer with lessons in immorality, splendour, the derailed aspects of *la vie de bohème*, and the importance of rich women. Already something of a pet in some quiet intellectual *salons*, Cocteau moved, with the great impresario, into the world of Misia Sert (a powerful beauty who, first as Madame Edwards and then as wife of the Spanish painter Jose-Maria Sert, financed and publicized much of Diaghilev's work), Coco Chanel (the wildly successful young *couturière* who took over Misia's burden when more funds were needed), and Madame de Greffulhe (Proust's Princesse de Guermantes, who had backed Diaghilev's first season in 1909). Bringing news of Montparnasse, Picasso, Modernism in its wildest forms to these ladies, Cocteau was rewarded with adoration, and the dinners, presents and gossip without which his developing sense of *pauvreté de luxe* was incomplete. It was in *this* world rather than in the world of giants like Braque and Picasso, or even blue-stockings like Gertrude Stein, that Cocteau created the sense of impromptu bohemia, cluttered with postcards, manuscripts and silk scarves, which surrounds him in countless photographs. Its women, who became his audience for a balancing act between society and modern art, changed from ground-length Worth tea-gowns to knee-short Chanel suits of sailor jersey, and, after the First World War, began a novel search for youth at Elizabeth Arden's beauty salon, skiing in St Moritz or dancing in cabarets full of black-tied lesbians or pomaded gigolos.

By 1918 Cocteau was at the nadir of his acceptance by either the avant-garde or the literary establishment, both of whom suspected him of belonging to the other camp (Cocteau's camp was, as time proved, uniquely personal, and he made it into what W. H. Auden called 'a warehouse, not a museum'). His *juste milieu* was, for a time, a well-to-do aristocratic one, into

125 An aristocratic Bohemian, Marie-Laure epitomized her own style in this photograph of her studio, the stark modernism of which contrasts eloquently with her Louis XV chair and Schiaparelli *tailleur*

126 The Dalis in Marie-Laure's collection referred to her Surrealist enthusiasms and the commissioning of *L'Age d'Or*; superb Goyas and eighteenth-century furniture in the house lent cachet to the avant-garde art

127 *L'Age d'Or* was perhaps the de Noailles' greatest piece of patronage, but it coincided with the commission for Cocteau's *Le Sang d'un Poète*. These divertissements created the scandal Marie-Laure adored but earned her husband excommunication and expulsion from the ultra-conservative Jockey Club

128 The Hôtel
Bischoffsheim, which
Marie-Laure inherited
from her grandfather,
supplied a courtly,
Trianon background for
Surrealist festivities, an
Aladdin's cave for
impoverished artists

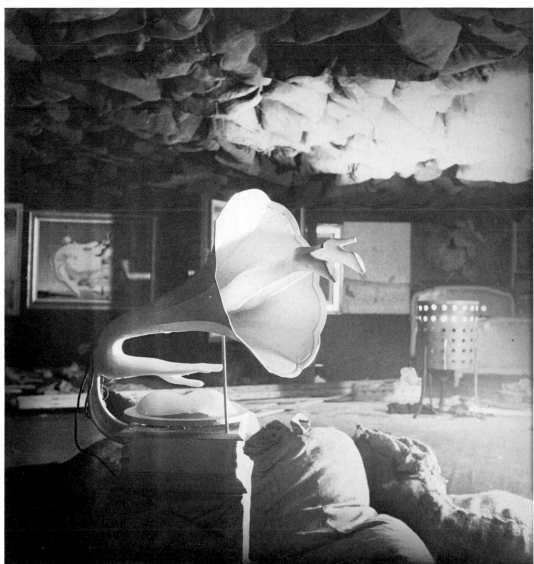

129 Oscar Dominguez,
whose object-sculpture
Nevermore featured
prominently at the 1938
Surrealist show, adored
Marie-Laure; she
responded with interest
and concern until the
painter's tragic suicide

130 Images of a vague, Goyaesque dream-world
came to Marie-Laure at her eighteenth-century
easel, among the priceless boiseries and amusing
knick-knacks with which it pleased her to
surround herself

131 Their Mallet-Stevens country house at Hyères (shown under construction) represented the de Noailles' modernism in its streamlined format: here, paradoxically, they lived and entertained with eighteenth-century grandeur

which he flew, with his lover Raymond Radiguet (first of his 'angels', twenty-year-old novelist, early casualty of France's Roaring Twenties), like an elegant bird of prey. His taste for magic secrets, cults of personality, the theatre, history and legend, as well as new clothes, elegant surroundings, old names, blossomed in a world lavishly possessed of all these things. Prominent among his affluent 'godparents' was Madame de Croisset, wife of a minor author and poet, widow of a fabulously wealthy banker – Bischoffsheim. Madame de Croisset was endowed with a double glamour for Cocteau's many snobberies: her mother was the model for Proust's Duchesse de Guermantes, and her maiden name was de Sade, a literary reference profoundly resonant in the milieu from which sprang Antonin Artaud and Surrealism. Visiting their house at Grasse, Cocteau met and was enchanted by a long-nosed girl with heavy dark hair, cut like Raphael's in his self-portrait – the daughter of the house, Marie-Laure Bischoffsheim.

Marie-Laure, who remained all of her life spell-bound by creativity and handsome young men, confided to her grandmother, 'When I'm fifteen years and three months old I'll marry Jean.' Madame de Sade, who, like most of her family, bore no resemblance to her infamous ancestor, must have discouraged Marie-Laure, who went on to marry the cultured, hand-some, titled scion of an ancient family: Charles, Vicomte de Noailles. Though this marriage, which seemed to take Marie-Laure far from the artistic, pharmaceutical and sexual anomalies of Cocteau's career, was very much of her mother's social level, it was also a great step to freedom. With it Marie-Laure, already a talented painter and intelligently curious about the arts, added to her immense personal fortune (she inherited the Bischoffsheim millions) a

132 The rehearsing of a concert under the conductor Roger Desormières, in the rococo ballroom of the Place des Etats-Unis mansion. The dissonances of modern music produced a frisson in contrast to such a setting

133 Perhaps the ideal
Surrealist interior would
have resembled this corner
of that movement's 1938
Paris exhibition; however,
in reality it was only with
Marie-Laure that stunning
contrasts of luxury and
bizarrerie coincided in the
true Surrealist manner

134 Dorothea Tanning,
*Chambre 202, Hôtel du
Pavot*. This installation
piece in the Centre
Pompidou preserves for
our generation the dream
transformation of ordinary
interiors dear to the
Surrealists and essential to
Cocteau's poetry and films

name renowned in eighteenth-century French history and twentieth-century French poetry.

Marie Antoinette's best friend as a distant ancestor, and cousin-by-marriage Anna de Noailles (the voluble Rumanian who published reams of heroic poetry and dominated Parisian society before World War One with a ceaseless monologue delivered from what, for twenty years, she called her deathbed), were stiff competition for a young wife determined, and expected, to cut a swathe in Parisian upper-crust circles. Marie-Laure compounded her obstacles with a heavy figure and curious, Assyrian looks not quite the right equipment for dazzling society in the era of flappers, short hair and beaded dresses. However, the de Noailles, both of them, rose to the challenge, going in for modernity and opulent patronage in a way which made their names, especially Marie-Laure's, synonymous with the brightest and best in the city of light for the next fifty years.

In Paris the de Noailles inhabited the Bischoffsheim mansion, a Ritz-style palace on the Place des Etats-Unis (a modernist touch which added to the cosmopolitan image they maintained); in the country they could choose between the Croisset house at Grasse, the exquisite Pavillon Pompadour, built for Louis XV's mistress at Fontainebleau, or the medieval ruin at Hyères, on which they had a plaster, glass and chromium house erected to designs by Robert Mallet-Stevens. The Paris house, by 1929, was a curious mixture of styles, containing most elements of French taste during the 1930s. A severely luxurious drawing-room decorated by the doomed Jean-Michel Frank, practitioner of an austere combination of crude materials and rare craftsmanship, dominated the house. The stairs and dining-room, however, remained in a hôtel-Louis XVI style stunningly contrasted with African trophies, Rubens tapestries, and enormous pictures by Dali (crushed automobile sculptures by César would join the fray during the 1960s). The newest thing in hot water, good reading-lamps, and superb service added to this bizarre mixture attractions which rarely failed to magnetize anyone Marie-Laure wished to entertain. Those of her guests who were most privileged also visited Hyères, where gym instruction (by what André Gide called a 'most agreeable young man'), swimming and sunbathing (the lot included in home-movies taken by Man Ray) were in order, to suit the ultramodern *mise-en-scène*. Rarer spirits appreciated the care and erudition with which Charles de Noailles restored and refurbished the Pavillon Pompadour, filling it with as many objects as possible which had belonged to its original owner.

The friends who enjoyed such sumptuous up-to-dateness were varied but artistic: Cocteau, first of all, and in his wake the *naïf* painter Jean Hugo; the imaginative and lovable Christian Bérard, neo-rococo painter and set-designer; architect, draughtsman and historicist Emilio Terry, film-star Jean Marais, Picasso. Marie-Laure's own, often wild personal enthusiasms attracted André Breton, Pope of Surrealism, Louis Aragon, the movement's greatest poet; Dali, and his less successful fellow painter Oscar Dominguez, with whom Marie-Laure had a long relationship, tragically terminated by his macabre suicide; the Broglies, Greffulhes and other titled figures of her mother's world, as well as Marie-Louise Bosquet, doyenne of Paris *Vogue*, Cecil Beaton, and the star-crossed young American composer Ned Rorem, with whom Marie-Laure had another peculiar, unhappy relationship. Such people spread a gospel of style to the four corners of Paris, if not the world; Marie-Laure was one of the prophets of this style, a hybrid gaiety as eclectic as her guest-book.

In 1929 the de Noailles gave a private screening of a film for which they had supplied sympathy and encouragement: it horrified their guests. *Un Chien Andalou*, a combined effort by Luis Buñuel and Salvador Dali, contained all the elements of horror, blasphemy and irrational logic which the public demanded of Surrealism. Even the Etienne de Beaumonts,

135 The ironic humour of the 1920s and 1930s is evident in Balthus's picture of Marie-Laure as a simply dressed girl in a stark chamber resembling a schoolroom attic

136 (*Left*) Salvador Dali, *Naissance de l'Ameublement Paranoiaque*, c. 1937. Dali's fantasia on Mae West's face (the sofa was actually made for several patrons) shows the fusion of traditional elegance and surprising detail with which Marie-Laure and her friends transformed their surroundings

137 Darling of many Parisian worlds, Christian ('Bébé') Bérard painted in a style derived from Raphael and Rose Period Picasso. Here his wistful charm and diabetic obesity are displayed before his frescoes *chez* Marie-Blanche de Polignac, a hostess who shared the art world with Marie-Laure

138 In Paris Marie-
Laure's poetic miasmas
had a palatial setting, the
whole scene evoking the
luxurious disorder beloved
of her Surrealist friends

139 Her human, bizarre but conventional stylishness and passion for the arts earned Marie-Laure a legendary place in the world of *vernissages*, concerts and feuds which made Paris so exhilarating between the wars

140 Cocteau's 'Bande' were rejuvenated and mythologized in his film *Les Enfants Terribles*. The beautiful kids playing at a tragedy in a half-empty mansion were his projection of the way Marie-Laure, her friends and Cocteau liked to imagine themselves

another artistic-aristocratic couple, well-versed in ballet patronage and avant-garde weird-nesses, were put out by the celluloid nightmare. Realizing that they had on their hands a social cynosure of a world miles beyond their tomb-like drawing-room, the de Noailles (prompted, one suspects, mostly by the distaff side) immediately commissioned two further films, a successor to *Un Chien Andalou* from Buñuel and, from Cocteau, a scenario which was at first to have been for an animated cartoon. Both commissions bore fruit in 1930, when the de Noailles themselves faced the fracas resulting from *L'Age d'Or* (Buñuel) and *The Blood of a Poet* (Cocteau). The anti-clerical *bizarreries* of the former earned Charles de Noailles a threat of excommunication from Rome and expulsion from the ultra-establishment Jockey Club; the scene where he and his wife, with guests, applaud a murder in the latter film might have provoked worse scandals, but Cocteau re-filmed it, replacing the aristocrats with transvest-ites and actors. In short, the two commissions catapulted the de Noailles to the head of the queue in modern art patronage, adding the glitter of shock value to their elegant worldliness.

The movies, music and films – all social arts – played a great part in Marie-Laure's generous but attention-demanding role as princess of bohemia. In her house Diaghilev's last protégé, the violinist Igor Markevitch, as well as Cocteau's hexagon of composers, *Les Six* (Georges Auric, Poulenc, Germaine Tailleferre, Arthur Honegger, Darius Milhaud, Louis

141 (*Left*) In England the taste of Edward James equated that of the de Noailles. Patron of Dali, Magritte and Delvaux, James filled his country house with such bizarre artefacts as this exuberant chair by Dali

142 A Louis XIV (whom she was said to resemble) to the arts, Marie-Laure fused the daring modernism of her Jean-Michel Frank drawing-room with the baroque taste of the late 1920s just as she mixed painters, poets and musicians in her social life

143 Elegant and supremely French, the *escalier d'honneur* of the de Noailles' mansion led – via paintings by Dali or the Vicomtesse herself – to the contrasts of a fantasy world

Durey), played their newest pieces; later Ned Rorem sang his simple, poetic settings of modern poetry; in the 1960s pop bands and Michel Polnareff graced the parchment-lined *salon*. Plain but intellectual-looking, like the Italian designer, Marie-Laure was the perfect foil for Schiaparelli's eccentric modes: jackets printed with newspaper clippings, sable coats with weight-lifter shoulders, barbaric jewellery all suited Marie-Laure to a tee. Under the liberating influence of Breton and Dali, Marie-Laure's own painting flourished, taking the form of blurred visionary tone-poems, with occasional bird-like figures, resembling Goya's *The Dog*. Such pictures, painted in a clinical studio by a Marie-Laure seated on a Louis XV *fauteuil*, wearing a tailored suit and a Dali jewel, conjure the discrepancies and harmonies of Cocteau's 'high wave' of style. The fairground rococo of Bérard's art, the costume parties given by the Beaumonts, Cocteau's and Giraudoux's modern-dress classic revivals in the theatre – all these were the elements of a style, not made-to-order, but collected, whimsically or passionately, for fun and because of love, by this extraordinarily sensitive woman. The neo-classical element of it all went perhaps too far in its French fashionableness (when both their own and Giraudoux's treatments of the Oedipus theme appeared in close succession on the Parisian stage, Gide exclaimed, 'It's an Oedipemic!'); Cocteau's *Orphée* and Beaton's photographs of Marie-Laure in mink among the same ruins which served as Death's kingdom in that film, and the sometimes cloying beggar-boys and sad clowns of Bérard or his friend Eugène Berman, were perhaps overly frivolous responses to the unrest and poverty of the decade which gave birth to Fascism. A certain amount of hobnobbing with the German high command during the occupation explained the fact that the de Noailles did not leave Paris, and remained unmolested, despite Marie-Laure's Jewish blood. The smear of collaboration does not seem to have touched the aristocratic couple, who, in the tradition of the royal courts of the eighteenth century or of a Montesquiou, felt themselves above politics.

Marie-Laure died suddenly and unexpectedly. She left no great collection, few paintings of great worth, no memoirs. Her role as an arbiter was an intensely twentieth-century personal effect, combining elevated interests with self-indulgence, financial power with human warmth, and aesthetic humility with social prestige. The throaty laugh with which she greeted human vagaries, identifying them perhaps with her own, is her most poignant legacy. The woman who served dinner calmly after *Un Chien Andalou* was still capable, in 1970, of replying to a story about a young man who had turned to street prostitution to make his living, despite numerous talents, 'I, I myself have walked the streets. They are full of wonderful people.' In meeting those wonderful people, finding out about them, indulging them – and herself with them – Marie-Laure de Noailles extended the last breath of aristocratic patronage into the age of movie moguls, glossy fashion magazines and nuclear war, lighting up the world which vanished with Hitler.

144 In baroque sunglasses by Giacometti, Peggy baptizes a new canvas on the canals of Venice. She brought a breezy modern extravagance to the city of aesthetes, provoking extreme reactions in the process

Peggy Guggenheim
1898–1980

The admired tone of the 1920s came to be a combination of those two opposing human motives which define Fashion: the need to conform and the need to rebel. If there was any ideal milieu for producing both these necessities in one person, it was the upper reaches of New York Jewish society in turn-of-the-century America. Peggy Guggenheim effortlessly personified the maddening and marvellous chaos from which 'modern art' was distilled between the wars. Her childhood, as the cosseted middle daughter of a union between finance and copper-smelting fortunes, left her fretting to break the rules of a stiff and pointless society, and self-consciously determined to maintain the secure platform of luxury and power which protected her from discomfort. Added to this she had a keen eye, lust (apparently inherited) on a prodigal scale, insatiable powers of hero-worship, and the shrewdness which had enabled both her immigrant grandfathers to become multi-millionaires.

These characteristics made her influential; surprisingly her influence was, in the long run, felt far more on the world she left behind her than on the European scene she adorned for so many years. In the same sense it is on the 1950s, not the 1920s when Peggy was at the height of her powers and formed her lifestyle, that her mark is most obvious. This lack of synchronization, so representative of art and life in postwar America, is indeed one of her greatest originalities. The arbiters of style have a certain divine madness among their strengths. The flame of anarchy and bohemianism which la Guggenheim kept alight throughout the war decade certainly prepared the art world for the revolutions of the Sixties as well as reminding it of those in the Twenties. If there was any Egeria for this mainstream of madness it was Peggy Guggenheim.

But why, one asks, and how? Peggy Guggenheim was not so very famous. Nor is her collection remotely as grand, permanent or even important as that of her uncle Solomon Guggenheim, housed in New York in the famous snail-shell building by Frank Lloyd Wright. It must be something about Venice, one thinks, and the somewhat louche impression she gave. Well, in the realms of taste Venice and an unsavoury reputation are excellent keystones for immortality. The ability to astonish, like Rumour, lies as much in what is said about one as what one actually does. Becoming a name to conjure with implies magic in the name, not the conjuror. More a prestidigitator than a conjuror anyway, Peggy Guggenheim so concentrated on the attempt to make her act work that she attracted an audience almost without asking for one. Any audience, whether they applaud or hiss, if their attention is held long enough will remember a performer. 'Miss Guggenheim' (something Peggy rarely was legally, but remained proverbially all her life) took centre stage, following Gertrude Stein in the file of middle-class dilettanti who utilized art in the search for self, replacing, during the 1920s and 1930s, the aristocrats who had played the same role through tradition and pride. Her novelty lay in allowing the role to be thrust upon her, much as rich ladies allow dressmakers to impose a 'look' on their wardrobe; in this she helped destroy the *fin-de-siècle* arrogance of self-appointed taste-makers, replacing it with a vulnerable extravagance which intensified the modernist love affair between art and money.

145 Franz von Lenbach painted the infant Peggy as a Van Dyck princess; she retained the royal manner, but behaved more like Catherine the Great

146 In Paris in the Twenties Peggy first set up as an exotic Poiret sultana. That the photograph was by Man Ray suggests the more up-to-date image she was shortly to attain

147 At Peggy's Art of This Century gallery in
New York, the designer Frederick Kiesler
utilized space brilliantly, creating for art a post-
Surrealist circus atmosphere with moulded
plywood, sailcloth and nautical grommets

148 Calder, Pevsner, Ernst and others showed to great advantage against the canvas walls and baseball-hat display stands in the gallery

Peggy Guggenheim is compelling in photographs. Changes in clothes and body – from the hobble-skirted Jewish débutante, through the awkwardly exotic lamé-clad Poiret mannequin or the Schiaparelli-suited *femme du monde* to the besandalled, kaftan-draped Byzantine Empress of her old age – are astonishingly superficial. Beneath them there remains unaltered the high-hipped skinny-legged adolescent girl, who stands ill at ease, staring into the camera with a look of squinting misery in her entirely vulnerable face. She can pose, as she does in the famous Man Ray shot of her wearing a Poiret Sultana outfit, but diffidently, as if threatened by the camera, fearful of the observing eye she, more than likely, had commissioned herself. It is perhaps this insecurity, obvious yet subtle, which made her so compulsively interested in looking at other people. She herself admitted that she searched constantly for a father to replace the handsome, devil-may-care figure she lost through his tragic death on the *Titanic*. As that death was occasioned by his return from an extra-marital adventure (which distressed Guggenheim *mère* enormously), the hint of sex linked to tragedy may have planted the seeds for Peggy's complicated and self-avowedly anguished love-life. In the great artists of her times Peggy found both father-figures and lovers; she is unique in having made her style out of a literal romance with art, to the extent that one is amazed to discover she had two children, while perhaps imagining that she had affairs with many more painters than she actually did.

149 (*Above*) Max Ernst. Peggy married the Surrealist genius ostensibly to save him from the holocaust of World War II. She also loved him, and suffered much anguish from his subsequent behaviour towards her in America. She remained a loyal patroness, despite his tendency to see women as dolls like these Hopi fetishes

150 Jackson Pollock, *Circumcision*, 1946. Despite some ingratitude on his part, Peggy was an early and generous supporter of Pollock, in whose work she saw a continuation of that abstractionism and weirdness she had appreciated in pre-war Europe

151 During the war years
spent in New York, Peggy
established her famous
gallery, the extraordinary
décors giving Americans a
fresh look at the future

Nevertheless, as a transmitter of ideas put by her lovers to an art-loving public, her list of achievements is outstanding. Married while she was still extremely young to one of New York's foremost bohemians, the writer, artist and madcap failure Laurence Vail, Peggy removed to Europe, where she and her husband set up a free-love free-for-all (except Peggy, who paid for everything) in the south of France and Paris. An early and continuing liaison with Marcel Duchamp (who was clever enough to understand her potential as a backer and fortunately preferred his ladies plain) introduced her to the Cubist-Dada-eventually-Surrealist world. Her point of view was not like Gertrude Stein's in any way. Modernity to Peggy Guggenheim was a thrill, a hunt for sensation, a social accolade – not an intellectual pastime. Somehow managing to be friends with characters as disparate as Emma Goldmann (the Jewish matriarch of Anarchy), Herbert Read (elder statesman of English anti-establishment thinking in the 1930s) and Antoine Pevsner ('more a mouse than a man', who nevertheless added greatly to the prestige of abstract sculpture), Peggy pursued with passion first Samuel Beckett, then E. L. T. Mesens, the Surrealist dealer, and finally Max Ernst, whom she married during World War Two. The achievements of all these men were ceaselessly exciting to her – Beckett's perhaps most of all, as she could not fathom his nihilism and his passion never equalled hers – and led to the formation of her important collection of modern paintings.

Throughout her residence in England (during which she divided her time between the country house where Djuna Barnes wrote *Nightwood* and her London gallery, Guggenheim Jeune), Peggy promoted Surrealism avidly. Through shared advertising expenses she helped finance shows by Magritte and Dominguez at Mesens' London gallery, while herself exhibiting Cocteau, Tanguy and Henry Moore. Her name was, during this period, synonymous with the most bizarre and avant-garde activities in London. Naturally she was never cultivated at all by conventional English society, which could certainly not have offered her the free association of artists and society to which France had accustomed her. It is not hard to see why, despite the collaboration of Herbert Read, Roland Penrose and Douglas Garman, she returned to the Paris of Eugène Jolas' magazine *transition*, Salvador Dali, and James Joyce. This was the milieu in which, intent on love, intrigue and art, she thrived until the outbreak of the war, cultivating artists of astonishing variety, with the aid of Duchamp, who introduced her to such disparate figures as Brancusi, Victor Brauner and Hans Arp. She bought art whenever the mood, the man or the manifesto suited her. Indeed, in her last days in Paris, at the beginning of the war, she resolved (and managed) to buy a painting a day until she left on the *Clipper* for safety and New York. Her arrival there, accompanied by her children, Max Ernst and his mistress, the painter Leonora Carrington, heralded a great stir in the art world, which might have been even greater if it had not been made in defiance of the prevailing wartime austerity.

With her she brought the heritage of a generation which had become legendary. But Peggy Guggenheim was no Fitzgerald heroine. Her Jewishness alone excluded her from the WASP never-never land of *Gatsby* and *Tender is the Night*. In 1942–3 she founded what she hoped would be her own personal museum of modern art, a gallery-showplace called 'Art of this Century', in which constantly changing exhibitions announced the emergence of Jackson Pollock and the Abstract Expressionists, as well as introducing to America Ernst, Klee, Kandinsky, Miró, Brauner, and Alexander Calder. The setting was a harbinger of Fifties modernism, with gumwood walls curving like those of the London underground in one room, sailcloth stretched from grommets floor-to-ceiling in another, and pictures displayed

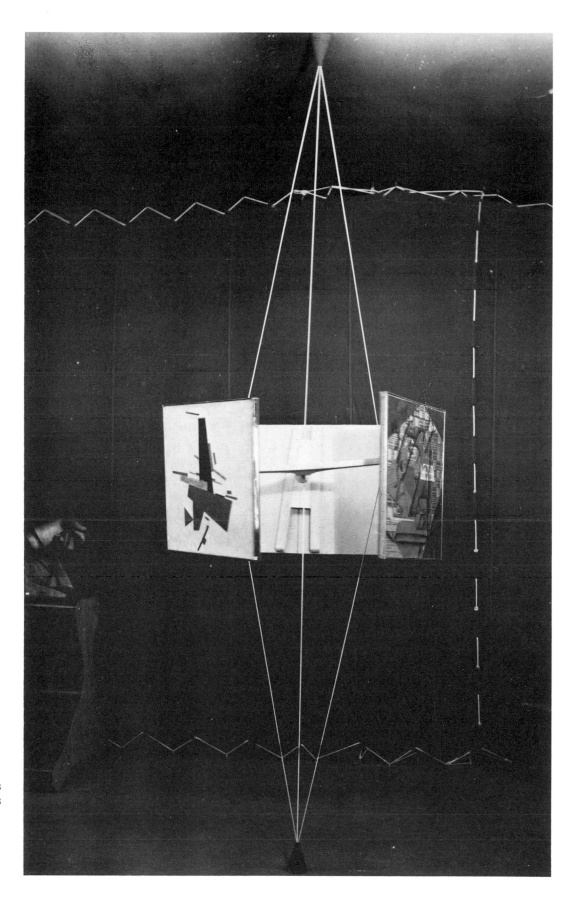

152 Astonishing even
today, Kiesler's ingenious
display stand for canvases
– based on a rope-held
sliding triangle –
epitomized pre-space-age
modernism in the new
gallery

153 The headboard in hammered silver by
Alexander Calder and her collection of earrings,
some by great artists, emphasized the intimate,
'shopping' aspect of Peggy's art enthusiasms

154 (*Above*) Palazzo
Venier dei Leoni: here the
Marchesa Casati
entertained, dressed by
Bakst and surrounded
with snakes and leopards;
here the scandalous Lady
Castlerosse drank and
charlestoned; here, finally,
Peggy Guggenheim
reigned as Empress of
Venice's art world.
Nicknamed 'palazzo non
finito', its air of hasty
abandonment perfectly
suited the great originals
who inhabited it

155 The Surrealist-
Functional aesthetic
predicted by Peggy's
collections and the décors
of Art of This Century
survived as hideous Fifties
kitsch style, quickly
superannuated by Sixties
Slick

156 (*Above*) A Giacometti torso and
Magritte's magical *Empire des Lumières* define
the eclectic ideals of beauty which dominated
Peggy's collecting

157 (*Left*) Yves Tanguy (photographed by
Man Ray in 1923), painter and Dadaist,
appealed to Peggy's sense of the outrageous
and focused her collecting on the Surrealist
world

158 Marino Marini, *The Angel of the Citadel*, 1948. Man and horse, ancient image of masculinity, found joyous expression in this bronze, whose phallus Peggy ordered to be made detachable to respect the feelings of passing nuns

on baseball-bats projecting from the walls, or against pieces of polymorphous heat-moulded plywood furniture which could stand on any of their three sides. Frederick Kiesler created this peculiar and imaginative décor, which continued the Surrealist concept of the gallery as a three-ring circus elaborately decorated, rather than an austere sanctum of the arts.

However, embittered by Jackson Pollock's lack of gratitude for her rewarding efforts on his behalf, and the lack of acceptance with which New York greeted her domestic and personal flamboyance (Ernst was with her during this period, though conducting many conspicuous alliances on the side, while many of her European cronies were in New York and doubtless visited her boudoir), Peggy returned to Europe in 1947. In Venice she acquired the unfinished ground-floor palace in which had lived the legendary Marchesa Casati, friend of Montesquiou and d'Annunzio, dressed by Bakst: the Palazzo Venier dei Leoni. Here at last she found a kind of peace, establishing her collection in its new setting, helping to fashion the Venice Biennale as we know it today, and continuing to astonish with her broad gestures and eccentric patronage. (Marino Marini's bronze horse-rider with an erection took pride of place in her courtyard; it is typical of Peggy Guggenheim's style that she had his member made detachable, as a gesture of conciliation to the horrified nuns who passed the spot; it was screwed on for gala occasions.) Not quite a museum, nor quite a private house, the Palazzo Venier dei Leoni became a mecca for art-loving Americans. Less high-minded than Greenwich Village, the Palazzo was the outward form of the wayward and bitter woman who was in a sense the Louise Brooks of Aristocratic Anarchy.

Exactly how all this reshaped the world around her is mysterious. But there are forms of art and decoration, as well as a kind of bohemian behaviour, which Guggenheim personified for three decades, or which were essentially 'in her style'. The mobiles of Calder, the more abstract works of Picasso, Duchamp's Dada *objets trouvés*, Giacometti's etiolated figures, Pevsner's wire and plexiglass abstractions, Jackson Pollock's splashes of genius – these, together with the denim-wearing conceptualists surrounding her friend John Cage, and the total nihilism of her adored Samuel Beckett, form a presage of the Greenwich Village style of the 1950s, the Beatnik style, as it was called, the masculine, un-chi-chi dishevelled world of the Abstract Expressionists. To read about the Village in the Fifties is like reading about Peggy Guggenheim's *ménages* in France, England and America throughout the century.

Not since the days of Reynaldo Hahn, Anna de Noailles and Whistler had Venice been such a magnet for the creative and the cognoscenti as she made it. Guggenheim's vast network of boyfriends, social acquaintances and financial dependants guaranteed many visitors to the Biennale once she lent it her prestige, and her collection. The Sixties and Seventies elected her an honorary Dogaressa of the city Gautier called *La Vénus de l'Adriatique*. The constant critical attention since accorded the Biennale has helped artists from Pollock to Hockney, and established the event as one of the major cultural pilgrimages of our times. An introduction to Peggy was a *sine qua non* of this pilgrimage. Under the circumstances the fact that Peggy continued to be essentially hospitable and gracious was remarkable. She did not tolerate fools, though, especially if they were unattractive to boot, and Pop Art made no dent on her essentially abstract sympathies in the visual realm. Fancying herself part of an historic revolt, she had no patience with other people's revolutions, and entered the embattled state of established eccentricity which comes to so many great taste-makers in their old age.

The fate of her collection is dubious, the permanent importance of her taste and patronage debatable. But her conspicuous generosity, her love (profound and physical) for art and

159 The interiors of Peggy's palazzo belied the classical
exteriors, providing contrasts between stark modern furniture,
luxury and expressive paintings: a museum for living in

160 Like a Pollock in cast iron and coloured glass, the landward gates of the Palazzo Venier (by Claire Falkenstein, 1961) seemed to lead to an abstract dream world, or to snare like a spider's web

artists, her flamboyant yet practical personality and her indefatigable powers of organization left their mark. Perhaps most importantly, she created a type of woman much emulated among the rich wives of American millionaires: aware of social position, but fascinated by bohemian Europe, dedicated unflaggingly if self-importantly to art, and endowed with those compulsions to hunt for, install and promote new finds which are more common to the men in American business dynasties. Every oil city, every banking capital, every industrial centre has its little Peggy Guggenheim; she founds the local museum, she cultivates the modern and fashionable; she collects primitive art or modern painting. If she is often unpleasantly tough, vain and uneducated, she nevertheless provides generous effluvia for the cultivation of the arts, and without her art would not have become as important as it has in modern America. Peggy Guggenheim often said she felt she was not 'a real Guggenheim' because her father's wayward career had prevented him – and her in turn – from inheriting real millions; instead she was a fairly well-off woman whom everyone imagined to be immensely rich. This taught her to use her wits. The clever way she utilized her reputation and her weaknesses by making her patronage more important than her expenditure opened the way for women from similar backgrounds to do the same. In the long run Peggy Guggenheim, more than anyone else, achieved what Wilde called (in a different context) 'the marriage of Romance and Finance'.

In 1959 Peggy published her expurgated autobiography *Confessions of an Art Addict*. Shortly before her death she wrote about her life since 1959, added it to the original narrative and published this disarming but louche account of her life again as *Out of This Century*. She linked old and new texts with a sentence which, in tone and text, accurately sums up her unique personality: 'I seem to have written the first book as an uninhibited woman and the second one as a lady who was trying to establish her place in the history of modern art.' It is fair to say she was both.

161 A light-industrial loft in mid-town
Manhattan, wallpapered in tinfoil, became the
centre of the Sixties: nightclub, sex parlour,
cinema, and studio for Warhol, ringmaster of the
Underground

Andy Warhol
b.1930

Among the figures who appear in this book, Warhol is the only seriously acclaimed artist; but so many people have made comments like Truman Capote's observation, 'I don't know exactly *what* it is that he's talented at, except that he's a genius as a self-publicist', that his position independent of the art world can be regarded as more important than his status as a painter. The very fact of this curious notoriety, which frankly uses celebrity status to turn any activity into Art, has established Warhol as a landmark in the history of Taste. Before him 'being an artist' meant, among other things, being yourself; since his debut it has come in some senses to mean 'being an Andy Warhol'. As a cynosure, Warhol has become a modern Marcel Proust, collecting, annotating, and appearing to define the fripperies and vices of his time and place, not for posterity but for today. This is a new role for the *arbiter elegantiarum*, one suggested by Cecil Beaton's retrospectively significant achievement as a diarist, but applied with the impersonal professionalism of an American businessman; such a novel combination of Saint-Simon and J. Pierpont Morgan has resuscitated the power of the VIP in an increasingly chaotic world; it has also partially restored to art the qualities of entertainment and education that it had during the Renaissance.

No more curious figure could have achieved this position, nor an apparent effortlessness which masks a fierce ambition. Born to Czech immigrants, raised in the polyglot squalor of Pittsburgh's mining environs, victim (he claims) of St Vitus' Dance, premature baldness and childhood bullying, with necrotic skin and silent lips paralysed with shyness – Warhol is an implausible figure which only the American system and peasant canniness could have guided to eminence. Trained at Carnegie Technical College, tried in the competitive world of New York fashion illustration, Warhol had acquired, long before achieving any artistic confidence, toughness, tact and the business acumen which distinguish him from the impractical and impoverished prototype of the bohemian artist. At the age of fifty-two he concocted his 'memoirs', which are in fact a carefully edited scrapbook created to augment an altered self and substantiate a myth. *POPism* is essentially the recollections of a homosexual ad-man; the book itself proves a point Warhol makes about an art-dealer friend:

I figured out he was such a successful dealer – it was because art was his second love. He seemed to love literature more ... Some people are even better at their second love than their first, maybe because when they care too much, it freezes them, but knowing there's something they'd rather be doing gives them a certain freedom.

This tallies rather well with Warhol's own famous declaration, 'I like boring things.' Such a phrase suggests, as does the book, that we can simply ignore Warhol's work in considering his life. He simply states when such-and-such a picture was done, flatly tells us why, and declines to analyse his preoccupation with mechanical, selfless reproduction. We can take it or leave it. If we take it as pure art, we are obliged to make those worrying links between Andy's pink and yellow cow-head wallpaper and the pastoral tradition since Constable, or between his home movies and the drawings of Gustave Doré, out of which Warhol's critic friends have done so

162 When Andy Warhol took up commercial art techniques in the service of gallery art he, ironically, revitalized the art of advertising. This boutique mural from London is a dim echo of the artist's 'Marilyn Monroe' silkscreens

well. Perhaps it is more in keeping with Warhol's own demands on his public to consider the manoeuvres by which his bizarre persona became a contemporary archetype.

Outside the masculine world of Abstract Expressionist painters, Warhol privately developed the taste for turn-of-the-century ephemera, the movies, and dandiacal perversity which Susan Sontag characterized in her famous 1962 *Time* magazine article on Camp. His own art was confined to Cocteau-esque book illustrations and witty fashion drawings. An avid collector of modern art, however, he saw the lessons to be learned from Jasper Johns's images of utilitarian objects; Warhol brought to this post-Duchampian aesthetic his own fey charm, a silent power of absorption, and a star-struck drive towards the already famous which were in tune with the social metamorphosis of the early 1960s. From these attributes stemmed a gambler's instinct to apply the camp sensibility with thorough conviction to lifestyle, creativity and publicity – an instinct which paid off in the already 'swinging' atmosphere demanding an arbiter. Passive receptor that he was, voyeur and borrower, Warhol suited ideally the post of Grand Improviser for which pop music, fashion and public taste were predisposed to nominate a candidate. To the tune of Bob Dylan's song *The times they are a'changin'*, the outsiders, hithertofore surly and defensively unacceptable, began to take over the imagination of Europe and America: whoever was willing to appear the weirdest, to provoke the most comment, to change most fluidly with the destruction of the *status quo* would automatically have been in the vanguard of this motley revolution. Roy Lichtenstein,

163 The essential conservatism of both Warhol
and his patrons is suggested by his biggest early
success as a painter: the flower series, a variation
in the mod mode on the traditional academic
flower-piece

164 Warhol's much-quoted phrase 'I like boring things' is contradicted by his cow wallpaper, which put art in an unlikely predicament and parodied 'environmental installations'

165 Curiously resembling
Warhol's friend and
Sixties *enfant terrible* Liza
Minnelli, these Carnaby
Street Christmas
decorations remind us that
much of the Sixties was as
tawdry in reality as was
Warhol's fantasy world

Mick Jagger, even Rudolf Nureyev were all candidates for the leadership, but each was too specifically a painter, a singer or a dancer to compete with Warhol.

Controversial though they were, Warhol's paintings did not make him avant-garde. Instead, it was the hint of his personality in the canvases, his famous friends, and what they wanted to think he was, which did the trick. First and foremost a solitary, an outsider, a climber, Warhol became the arbiter of a generation obsessed with elegance itself as an art-form. Without filming, taking pictures or writing, Warhol was thus able to anticipate an audience for carefully marketed movies, photographs or books which placed him in the world of *Vogue* while at the same time altering that world. All at once, without effort, Andy had become the new, hipster Cecil Beaton.

Warhol did not make the lifestyle which emerged in the 1960s; he didn't even create much of his acknowledged part of it. Other people made his silkscreen paintings, covered his studio with silver foil, dubbed it 'the Factory' (thus creating a new genre of blue-collar chic), improvised in front of his cine-cameras, published his magazine. But, like a brain in a science fiction film, he stood at the centre of all this activity, allowing ideas to ricochet off his impassivity straight into the glare of media publicity. By example he masterminded the whole transformation of art into something that *happens*, rather than something you *do*. The glittering décors of discothèques and the nostalgic clutter of young people's eclectic collections suited his own colder and older tastes, so he appeared in places where other artists his age might not have gone. The shrieks and nerve-crises of drug-addicts were not unlike the movie-star histrionics he had read about obsessively as a child, so he allowed the system of

166 The hemline wars of the Sixties were the kind of camp hangover from Fifties style that Warhol adored. These King's Road models display the full range of possibilities during the decade of '*the girl*'

167 The 1971 Kubrick film of Anthony Burgess's novel *A Clockwork Orange* epitomized all the trends the book had predicted for the 1960s. The outrageous marriage of urban violence, totalitarian politics and plastic chic lurking in the period re-emerged in the 1970s

underground 'superstars' to form around him, and committed their excesses to film with deadpan amateurishness. The increasing violence of rock music's throbbing popular pulse appealed to his concealed sexuality and was related to the charleston frenzy of the 1920s, about which he had a camp enthusiasm, so Warhol worked to background music supplied by the hit-song radio stations. But most of all, the antics of far-out kids, the shock of new art, the whiff of sex and drugs in the air seemed to appeal to the media and to the rich glamorous society who always follow the fashions first; this was the audience the immigrant boy wanted, the friends the fey aesthete desired, and the glamour the minor fashion draughtsman envied. Loneliness, frustration and snobbery are a forceful combination of motives. In Warhol their convergence mutated strangely into a productive phenomenon which seemed to create Pop Art single-handedly, although, as art, that movement was woven together of many other threads.

The influence of all this on public taste was uncanny. Warhol's snobbery, and his tastes, were fortunately shared by people like Henry Geldzahler, a rising curator in the Metropolitan Museum of Art, and Diana Vreeland, editor of New York *Vogue*. These people were respectively young enough and old enough to see Andy, who maintained a certain social conservatism throughout the wild decade, as an acceptable avant-garde stepping-stone, useful in a museum career for one-upmanship, and in fashion for appearing *à la page*. His name and those of his 'discoveries' were thus linked in print with the serious acquisition of modern art by public collections, and the breathless dissemination of daring couture collections. As both of these avenues led to very big business, Warhol acquired the

168 (*Left*) Promoting Warhol's slice of nightlife novel *A*, an assemblage of his aides and superstars provides an encyclopaedic selection of alternative personae for the next generation of rebels: Joe Dalessandro, Undine, Paul Morrissey, Viva, Ultra Violet, Louis Waldon . . . the outrageous in pursuit of the inimitable

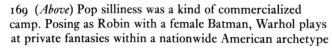

169 (*Above*) Pop silliness was a kind of commercialized camp. Posing as Robin with a female Batman, Warhol plays at private fantasies within a nationwide American archetype

170 (*Right*) Pop dealt in clichés, and never more so than in Warhol's studio. Elvis Presley, in gold paint, and a transvestite in black taffeta summed up his tinsel view of the consumer society

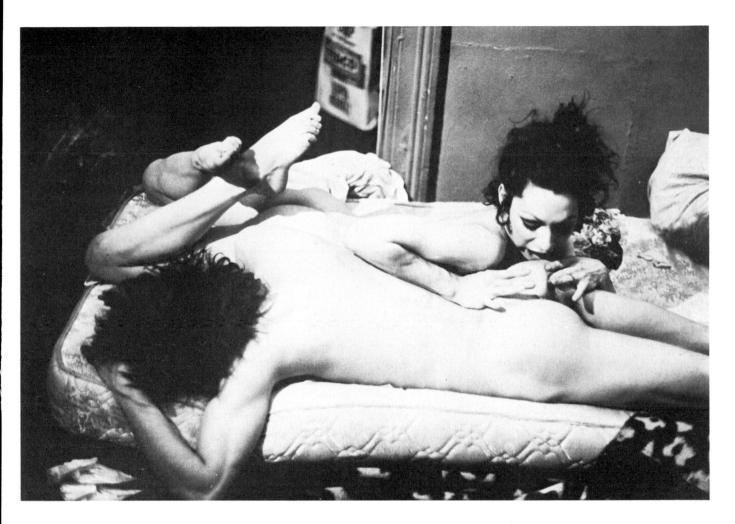

171 Warhol was in part responsible for the stylishness of sexual politics during the Sixties and Seventies – but films like *Women in Revolt* suggest that his interest was in part ironic, in part voyeuristic. These figures are both men

opportunity to market his work, invest his profits, and continue his celebrity as if it had always existed. His genius lay in knowing how to do these things, and in his lack of self-consciousness about the stylistic volte-face. Though daily fare in the so-called rag trade, abrupt changes of interest and friendship are less respected in an artist. However, Warhol, suiting the media-imitative psyche of the Sixties, made such switchbacks essential to his creative persona: he made movies with beautiful girls (Jane Holzer, Edie Sedgwick, Brigid Polk) or boys (Joe Dalessandro, Tom Hompertz), and dropped them when their demands for money or attention exceeded his need for them. He painted linear works depicting Campbell's soup cans (1962), switched to silk-screened news clippings in repeating rows (1964), and then turned to celebrity portraits in a technique combining photography and line-drawing (1968). He changed from photographer to film-maker to publisher of *Interview*, a society gossip magazine which stands in relation to the powerful *Women's Wear Daily* as the *Village Voice* stands to the *New York Times*. He altered his appearance from leather-clad bohemian to white-tied society figure to preppy godfather. In short, he continued to be an indecisive figure, intent on personal satisfactions beyond our comprehension, but in so remaining appeared the quintessence of twenty years' kaleidoscopic taste.

Two aspects which emerge clearly in retrospect as essential to Sixties style are the Night-time habits of the pop figures and the Daytime modernism of the Alternate people. Although they overlap, recurring in the Glitter Rock explosion of the 1970s, and the concurrent back-

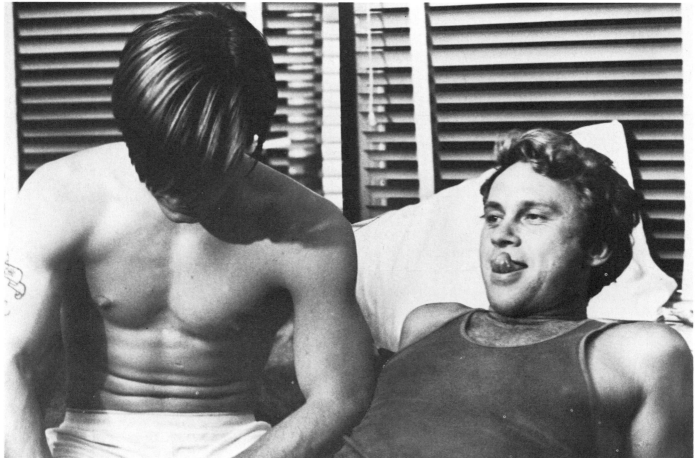

172 (*Left*) If the Warhol world condoned any real form of interior decoration it was the frantic hodge-podge assemblage of druggie poverty, parodied in this scene of chaos from the underground film *Loves of Ondine*

174 (*Right*) From white plastic stylishness the Sixties (as drugs caught on with their attendant *laissez-aller*) turned to old clothes, an imitation pre-Raphaelitism, and general shagginess in taste. The Rolling Stones linked revolt and romanticism in a successful bid for riches and fame

173 (*Left*) In contrast with his promotion of transvestite glamour Warhol filmed Joe Dalessandro, the perfect American body-builder, as an equally sleazy macho stereotype. The Venetian blinds and underclothes in this still from *Flesh* remind us of the English pop painter David Hockney's domestic genre scenes

175 A perverse and tragic chic became attached to drug-taking in the Warhol milieu: it burnt out many of the trend-setting beauties he exploited. A still from *Flesh for Frankenstein*, 1973

176 (*Left*) Chairman of trendiness the world over, Andy Warhol pays tribute to his obsession with the instantly recognizable by means of a multiple image of Mao Tse-Tung

177 (*Below*) This still from Warhol's *Blood for Dracula* – a 3D vampire film released under his name – suggests the accusations of parasitism the artist has suffered, as well as the socialite environment attained by his world

to-the-earth fashions, these two attitudes commenced, respectively, about 1962 and 1967. Andy Warhol's two studios, the old and new factories, reflect both styles: even the windows were covered with the ubiquitous aluminium paper in the dimly-lit early factory, where disco music, mirrored reflectors and non-stop partying were the order of the night; after the 1968 attempt, by a crazed feminist, to assassinate the President of Pop, Warhol moved to another studio on Union Square, where intercoms, white typewriters, polished wooden floors and daylight took over from the vampire aesthetic of druggie culture. These shifts of décor also underline Warhol's own jumps in status, away from the underground cult image which launched him, into the streamlined up-to-dateness which had become the norm among the art-world establishment. But what was the art world then? It had come to be a loose geography, including rock-star socialites like Mick and Bianca Jagger, established curators like Geldzahler or London's Roy Strong, writers like Tom Wolfe or even Norman Mailer, and fashion personalities varying from Penelope Tree (daughter of the US Ambassadress to the United Nations) to David Hockney (the English painter who seized on the late arrival of Pop Art in England to launch himself in the world of glossy magazines). This milieu was no longer based on the subjective values of brushwork and canvas, and no longer dictated to by the studious pronouncements of cultured aesthetes; it was a world of journalism, but without a house paper, played out for TV cameras or gossip grapevines, where success depended on huge advances against minimal output, arbitrary scandals about drugs, sex, or taxes, and a first-name greeting from the other members of the cast. The nature of art, what we expect from it, or from its practitioners, changed with all this, and Warhol can be said to be, if not the cause, the catalyst for the transmogrification.

Like Lady Mendl, Warhol is a colossal snob, a fantastic self-promoter, and has disguised his middle age by adopting silver-dyed hairpieces which photograph as youthfully blond; he practises cosmetic excesses which, like Lady Mendl's exercises and facelifts, do not make him so much younger-looking as timeless. His appeal, like hers, consists of the charm of 'yes', the profitable agreeableness of the trivial-minded and the outsider. It is due to the admiration and eventual participation of such determined and adoring *arrivistes* that Society, whatever it is, can continue to call itself Society, and Warhol is the newest cup-bearer among the deities. The point of his art, his taste and his personality is not what he did or why he did it, but that, true to the American Dream, HE GOT THERE. Any sense of humour about himself as he looks back at his career is an accident among the pages of parties, famous names, stars, events, all described with a deadpan idolatry. The deadness is explained when we realize that, in words and pictures, Warhol expects us to be as impressed by his world as he is; he doesn't need superlatives, he *is* one. The title of his book, itself a piece of Pop Art, sums up his heritage thus far: **POP**, in bold letters, proudly declares his personal, world-famous invention; *-ism*, in lower case, humbly and self-deprecatingly apologizes for all the fuss, and soothes his famous acquaintances with a suggestion that all this art stuff is a bit of a joke. Perhaps it is.

Malcolm McLaren
b.1946

M/McLaren

In the 1960s the British equivalent of Warhol's promotion of transvestites and drug-chic outsiders was an enthusiasm about working-class styles and tastes. Prejudice in America, stylistically speaking, has usually been sexual or financial in its bias; the avant-garde opposes the establishment by the same criteria. In England, prejudice has always been based on the class system, supported by language and dress habits, as well as by neighbourhood and education. Opposition to the pin-striped, King's English-speaking upper and middle classes has therefore, since the days of the music halls, or Noël Coward's cockney sketches, been couched in the nasal unaspirate whine of the working-class Londoner. The hippie free-for-all of the Sixties embraced the sexual and stylistic tensions between the classes, elevating East End Londoners to rock stardom, making their language a universal one and, in some cases, borrowing workmen's clothes for the fancy-dress fashions of the decade. The gypsy caravan passed by, however, leaving a broader gulf between the poor and the rich than had previously existed; the permanent change in style occasioned by the Sixties revolution in America was not for neo-Elizabethan England. The unrest and unsolved stylistic riddles left behind by this period vanished for a few years in the Glitter Rock-based styles – Los Angeles mirror-and-low-sofa décors, platform shoes, makeup for men, all flotsam from the Pop world – and surfaced in a chaotic upheaval which came to be called New Wave, or Punk.

Surly, accidental, improvisatory, the members of this 'revolt into style' (as George Melly titled his book on the previous generation) acknowledged no leaders. However, Punk was based very much on the publicity coincident with rock recording, and on the responses of trendy fashion retailers and salaried journalists (or their researchers). This situation pre-supposes the presence of *eminences grises*; if the eminently visible movement had an impresario, it was Malcolm McLaren, who made anti-style into business.

An impish red-head, canny, sharp, and dissolute in appearance, McLaren trained as a cutter in the garment industry. His origins were thus entirely in the world of labour and commerce. His instincts for successful publicity and profiteering were acquired in the fashion business, at however humble a level, by osmosis: no contemporary milieu supplies a more compulsive drive to combine taste-making and commercial acumen. The toughness of life in the Rag Trade, amorphous but fiercely competitive, was an ideal platform to support the rebellion of the so-called 'uneducated classes'.

Forming a dynamic partnership with his girlfriend Vivienne Westwood, McLaren opened a shop at the unfashionable end of London's King's Road (called, for its remoteness from middle-class Sloane Square at the other extreme of the Road, World's End). Low rent may have motivated the choice of site, but it made an effective statement of disdain for the left-over Sixties chrome and neon of Chelsea's smarter shops. First catering to Teddy-boy rock-and-rollers (when the shop was called, in homage to James Dean, 'Too Young to Live, Too Old To Die'), McLaren attracted a wider audience of teenagers who wore the only style they had, and derived it from pop music. When Skinheads (tough street-boys whose shaven heads and workboots referred to the uniforms of the Borstal corrective institutions) and other rock

178 Combining fetishes and fashions, Malcolm McLaren backed as much as created the street and club changes in taste of the 1970s to emerge as the Diaghilev of Punk

179 The sexual menace, outrageous costume and truculent
pride in being an outcast that were essential to the Punk spirit
are perennial Cockney attributes: Anthony Burgess pinned them
down for ever in *A Clockwork Orange*

180 The *Clockwork Orange* stereotypes, wearing their shaven heads and work-boots in proud reference to the costume of delinquent remand homes, re-emerged as an avant-garde in the light of McLaren's advertising. Graffiti were so much a part of the style that they shortly became an Art

181 The author's portrait of Richard Hell, original member of the ultra-Seventies rock band TV, shows the taste explosion he personified for what he christened 'the Blank Generation'

182 Perversity became the norm in post-Punk London – if only for the benefit of the camera. Such antics might attract agents and the risc to famc and fortune heralded by McLaren's sponsorship of unexpected rock groups

sub-cults began to frequent the shop, it changed its name to 'Let It Rock', specializing in sharp sunglasses, tight jeans, fluffy sweaters and pointed shoes – in direct reference to the nifty early days of pre-hippy rock-and-roll. The change of name was a sign of the times: young kids in an increasingly impoverished Britain wanted an oracle, not a shop, a gathering-place where they could feel unified, stimulated and *safe*. For the fun of the thing and for the business, McLaren became the Marie-Laure de Noailles of this dole-queue generation (and their more affluent contemporaries in search of new fashions); his shop became their *salon*.

Like a *salon* McLaren's shop attracted writers and artists, but, true to its time, it attracted artists who were more interested in being in the vanguard of 'what's happening' than in objective creativity, and writers whose primary aim was earning a living by self-promotion in periodicals. In this sense the whole developing taste of London Punk, and to a certain extent its New York equivalent, was an exercise in window-dressing, perpetuated by hairdressers (soon to come into their own in the New Wave), art students (always keen to look as avant-garde as the art they would like to create) and older art-figures (eager to appear as young as they had been in their Sixties heyday, or simply attracted to this sexy new mode of dress and behaviour). When McLaren changed the shop's name – by now like a newspaper headline – to 'Sex' he gathered up the threads of New York rock style, left lying about by older figures like Lou Reed, or such dynamic young wastrels as Richard Hell or Debbie Harry, and wove them into a novel banner, under which a startling army quickly mustered.

'Sex' sold clothes based on fetish garments, previously kept in suburban closets. Leather, rubber, chains and zips composed an armoury of pornographic offensiveness which a

183 (*Far left*) Muscle was never much part of Punk (beer, drugs or glue-sniffing took their toll): but the 'Road Warrior' character (from *Mad Max II*) put a touch of heroism to the costume of defiant despair McLaren was marketing to London poor

184 (*Left*) Another shot from *Mad Max II*: these Australian films transformed Heavy Metal clothing and Hell's Angels morality into an aesthetic of violence which encouraged and derived from Punk images in England and New York

185 (*Left*) Not androids, but McLaren's living shop-window dummies, the Punks re-invented revolution with bits and pieces of comic books, sado-masochism and rock-n-roll. History will never know if McLaren's shop 'Sex' was the test-tube or the baby

186 The Sex Pistols ended up as horrific as people thought they were: they started out with the improvisatory offensiveness of the young in transition

187 'Sex' (a.k.a. 'Seditionaries') made the word
'bondage' acceptable – even to those who weren't
sure what it meant beyond the fashions created
by Vivienne Westwood. The matching Tartan
beer can is a nice touch of Punk chic

188 Following up Punk was difficult: elements of Marilyn Monroe, Dracula and Barbarella appeared in costumes designed to attract attention (and fame?) at new nightclubs

dissatisfied younger generation took to enthusiastically. The older citizens of London or New York, who may have seen such clothes in sex clubs or their private collections of erotica, were as surprised as the conventional parents at this sudden eruption from an underground the kids cannot ever have been part of. McLaren's marketing genius was responsible for this. As an arbiter he anticipated his audience, sensing that further extremes, carried on from the leather-jacketed, fishnetted, vaguely kinky personal style of the Warhol stars, were in order; adding to this outrageous elements of gay sex-costume, and all the clichés of the professional prostitute's wardrobe, he created a purchasable sense of daring. In these clothes, or listening to the Sex Pistols, a band McLaren promoted to advertise his shop, 'punks' – as they began to be called in 1976 – could feel, not only a genuine sense of alienation, caused by poverty and class, but the *frisson* of the pervert, the lover of forbidden things. That these sensations were more often than not cancelled by an extensive use of pricey sedatives (heroin was accorded a cultist glamour more widespread than its underground cool had been in the Sixties) or cheap knock-outs like commercial glue was not apparent to the shocked bystander. Anti-establishment songs (the Sex Pistols' record *God Save the Queen* was banned on British radio

189 (*Left*) Many of the things vaguely appreciated in the Sixties – pop art lettering, ripped cloth, perverse leather, short hair, bizarre long hair – were organized by McLaren into specific (also rather expensive) units of style for a generation that felt it had missed the exciting decade

190 Inheritors of Punk unrest, The Clash carried working-class British militancy into the rock vocabulary, adding a touch of seriousness to the perverse follies of McLaren's youth styles

stations), anti-classical advertising (shattered print and badly reproduced images torn from newspapers created punk graphics), and, most enduringly, anti-traditional haircuts (the phallic nudity of the skinhead was dyed orange or green, the crested Mohican towered above pedestrians, and the lacquered black vampire pompadour made hookers of schoolgirls) – these were the tactics by which McLaren brilliantly (and cheaply) turned the streets of London into a runway, and unemployed kids into his models. Punk was, in that sense, a great fashion show, as much as anything *chez* Dior or Cardin, with the aim, not only of changing styles annually, but of making money by doing so.

McLaren himself has just the right combination of pugnacious offensiveness, self-possession and professional expertise to pull all this off. His style is not domestic. His forté is 'appearing', quietly dressed, in public – but at moments when his *protégés* create scandals as memorable as the Sex Pistols' signing of a record contract, in all their offensive finery, outside Buckingham Palace. Like Warhol, he is an ear, and a pair of eyes which absorb, refashion, and promote. The actual designing skills in his business lie with Vivienne Westwood, whose interest in fabric, cut, shape, and the other components of fashion have made punk and later clothing, if not durable, unforgettable. Her flair and lively sense of fun created the neo-romantic backlash to punk in 1980; while McLaren promoted the singer Adam Ant, Westwood launched the new regency styles, braided, breeched and piratical, which were supposed to sweep away the now ubiquitous kinky kids. If this style was not entirely popular (resembling as it did the Sixties dressing-up against which McLaren had originally aimed his fashion revolution), it cleared the air for a hybrid style, at once romantic and sleazy, which has dominated London ever since. At the end of a new wave, the sex rockers have found a free-for-all style, assembled from rags and couture cast-offs, sinister and decorous at the same time, which coincides with the new name of McLaren's shop: World's End.

The partnership which promoted this change in lifestyle has been reported as on the point of dissolution. 'World's End' is a valuable, and hotly contested, brand name in the fashion business. McLaren has been, since the Sex Pistols, better known as a promoter of rock bands than as a stylistic trendsetter – Adam and the Ants, Bow-Wow-Wow, and the Sex Pistols have each outlasted the modes they were conjured to support. He is now a celebrity in his own right, having achieved that visibility which is the paid profession of a self-elected taste-maker in our time. Whatever he comes up with next will simply be another exemplar of the unique shift in the role of the arbiter he represents. From the justified commercialism of Warhol, McLaren has moved the selection of new tastes into the realm of frank, unembarrassed commerce. His 'style war', as it has been rather pretentiously termed, was not a war; instead, by appearing to be, it sold the soldiers what they wanted. Put less metaphorically, he sold the working-class dissidents of London the uniforms they had first devised for themselves, from dreams, imitations of idols and things which perhaps frightened even them. The militant aim of all this immensely stylish offensiveness was belied by the simple fact that one of McLaren's names for his shop was 'Seditionaries'. You cannot call a shop a revolution simply because it is named 'Revolution'. However, despite the calculated, or, from another point of view, despairing soullessness in this essentially fashion-oriented attitude towards style, McLaren's efforts helped to detonate an explosion which cleared the air for many new developments in the arts.

If Malcolm McLaren were run over by a bus today (or drowned in the Amazon, where in 1983 he went in search of the ancient sounds and sights which he feels our society to be badly in need of), his heritage would be indefinable: no art, no books, nothing but proprietorship of

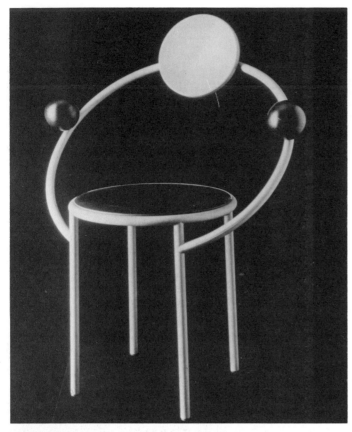

191 The self-consciously mad futuristic look of the Eighties inherits Pop gimmicks and Punk harshness: under the guise of an eclectic neo-classicism this style has scored great success for the Milan-based design group Memphis. The chair is by M. de Lucchi, 1983

192 Tiger-skin, leopard-skin, zebra-skin – Fifties chic, circus tackiness, Hollywood glamour and many other levels of style rendered these (always false) furs fashionable throughout the Seventies. These sheets from a London shop, Practical Styling, recall Punk trousers and rock-n-roll jackets

193 The sleaze of vinyl gained cachet from
McLaren's kinky clothes; the Practical Styling
shop married Punk to High Tech and purveys a
décor to suit the grab-bag of youthful taste

a shop and his name on some record sleeves. However, in the clothes of the last decade, in the art of graffito painter Keith Haring, in the sexual/political prose of Kathy Acker, in the witty iconoclasm of Memphis furniture – in all the bright or black decorative details with which we are currently inundated by the media, there would be a trace of him. McLaren did not make, inspire or even know about many of these productions – or countless others related to them which are about us as we awake daily – but in the urban aliens among whom he found his market-place he planted a seed, for whatever reason, which led to a change in receptivity.

In a sense all modern taste is a response to publicity, advertising and the media. Through the mere coverage, not to mention the virulent editorial opinion, accorded McLaren's ventures by these organs, our own points of satiety have been extended. Things have become stylish which were horrible a few years ago; the speed with which McLaren changed his shop, and its name or stock, did not cause this shift: it predisposed us, the purchasers, to make it ourselves. In that sense the phenomenon of Malcolm McLaren's London publicity campaign, and its success, is a landmark for our times: however depressing or cynical the

194 In the wake of Punk neo-expressionist trends from New York's *Zeitgeist*, painters filtered through to the London nightclub scene. One of the trendy dives – the Wag Club – acquired mural decorations suitable for the new Berlin

195 From Bow-wow-wow in this photograph to Boy George was a small step professionally but a larger one culturally, involving the rejection of McLaren's vaunted primitivism in favour of urban camp

196 Seeing the jungle in the city, McLaren promoted another rock group with the graffiti-based montage of neighbourhood bits and pieces he hoped to launch as the style of the Eighties

197 Normal clothes, unexpected Chicano sound: McLaren brought the ubiquitous New York Latin rock sound in the form of Rocksteady Crew to England as a novelty, symbolized by the portable stereo as heraldic device. The revolution is over

styles he represented may appear in retrospect to have been, they were not dictated by him, but sold in direct response to a democratically generated need in a new generation. That generation called itself, after a song by poet/singer Richard Hell (whose ripped T-shirt is said to have been the original paradigm of punk style) 'The Blank Generation'. Ironically, it filled in the blank with more style and invention than the world of taste has seen for half a century. There is no looking back.

Conclusion

De Gustibus Non Disputandum

The 1880s were a period of confusion and development in the arts and sciences. Arts and Crafts, historicist, functional, Italian, Gothic, Greek, Dutch – the styles of architecture and interior decoration were as numerous and hotly debated as the nuances of fashion. Pre-Raphaelitism in painting went through its second stage, furiously opposed by Academic neo-classicism or mediocre genre pictures. Oscar Wilde delivered lectures on reforms in dress which advocated a return to Romanticism in male attire, and uncorseted draperies for the ladies; Lord Salisbury, Disraeli or even Whistler were, on the other hand, committed to the severe black and white elegance born in the wake of Beau Brummell. Swinburne's wild, erotic onomatopoeia contrasted with Alfred Tennyson's escapist melancholy in poetry, while the young novelist George Moore advocated a French-style realism as antidote to the sentimental romances of the day. In France Paul Verlaine, the poet, Gustave Moreau, the painter, and Auguste Rodin, the sculptor, explored the misty realms of the subconscious, calling it the soul, and laying the foundations of Symbolism. In America and Germany a thirst for culture, indiscriminate in its avidity, balanced a frenzied commercialism and prosperity. Across the globe mechanical inventions – electric light, the telephone, the transatlantic telegraph, oil paints in tubes, more sophisticated sewing-machines – seemed to promise an infinite development of culture and novelty. Against this pattern of change, the depressing monotony of poverty, domestic hypocrisy and the ubiquitous frumpiness of residential décors alleviated a fear of the new.

The adage that history repeats itself is not a popular one with scholars. However, the progress of the last two centuries, each beginning with intellectual revolution and devastating warfare, provides parallels in the development of public taste which are fascinating. Our own era of the 1980s is also a period of fecund sterility, choked with stylistic conflict in the arts, apparently buoyed up by scientific discoveries, and threatened by social unrest and economic failure. Streamlined modernism, pastiche 'tasteful' and eclectic post-modernist schools of architecture clash in the illustrated periodicals. The dullest conventional clothing, for men and women, is worn alongside the wildest fetish garments and pseudo-poverty costumes, or the most expensive revivals of styles from the recent past. Music, at its most popular, appeals to opera-lovers, in the cinema and on stage, as well as to fans of bands making sounds with electric drills and industrial girders. Writing provides escapism in best-selling romantic novels of success and sex, but also brings us the poetry of psychopathy or the nostalgia for a past we did not know. Costly magazines preach, less wittily than Oscar Wilde, conflicting modes of interior decoration as if they were creeds of faith, playing on the sense of insecurity that has arisen in the gulfs between the capitalized rich and the socialized poor. In Britain, not one but *two* women rule in the idolized manner of Queen Victoria (the one providing her glamour, the other her conservatism); in America a jovial capitalist has brought back the freebooting style of the 1880s to the White House. How, among all these pressures, can we feel a personal effect?

We can learn the lesson which, in their determined, often egomaniacal way, the personalities in this book preached and practised: to think, to respond, to *see* are the noblest

198 From Rock to Rags,
McLaren and Westwood
countered their own
skintight modes (in the
best Paris tradition) with a
Dickensian hobo look that
seemed easier than Punk
but cost more

prerogatives of the human soul. Arrogant, conceited, biased or ridiculous, all these taste-makers followed the lead of their senses and interpreted the impulses they received from their imagination, in an attempt to change their own lives and those of their contemporaries. This act, pleasure and travail as it is, constitutes the single infinitely renewable moral alternative to fear, conformism and staleness. Our century has seen the chrysalis of aristocratic selectivity open into the democratic flowering of stylistic freedom which confuses and delights us today.

While this broad-based sense of personal choice has often failed to create beauty, contributing to the death of individual craftsmanship and sterility in official art, it has educated the eyes of the common man to a greater extent than ever before. *We* are the taste-makers of today, in the sense that we elect our arbiters through commercial processes. This may not be the pure ideal of Athenian democracy, but it does offer a diversity and responsibility for the world around us which was previously, like political power, thought to lie only in the hands of a few privileged souls. It may be true that the real forward steps in the arts will continue to be made only by individual personalities, and that these steps may also be noticed only by a small, carefully-attuned audience; however, through our thirst for the media and our increased receptivity to a torrent of information, *we* will follow those steps towards new styles with a march brisker and braver than has ever been possible. The personal effects which our decade can inherit or bequeath will be multiples of unique creations, sudden whims, or planned novelties – multiples on a scale up to now unknown. *We* are a vast market-place, a numberless audience, who can and do guarantee that the artist, poet or thinker, though misunderstood, need never starve ignored. *We* are the hunger and the thirst for beauty, direction and truth. *We are* the personal effect of what has come before us, who, if we can oppose a joyous stylistic freedom to the holocaust which threatens us, will emerge – however demanding the effort – *free from style*, as from fear.

In the true democracy of the fifth-century Athenians, the fripperies of the mode paled beside the concepts of truth, strength, beauty, and, most importantly, appositeness which were ingrained in the language and skills of the people. The dignity of the object, the verity of basic purpose, the literalism of faith and interpretation were all implicit in acts of creation and remain today, for all to see, in statues, architecture and philosophy. In our broader democracy, such virtues may again become possible. While the styles of our time appear to embrace dullness (as in American-style suburban architecture) or decadence (as in the neo-hobo vampire clothes of London's teenagers), the important point is that style is assumed to be an essential act of faith. The clothes, books, music, pictures bought today are acquired for a moral purpose, to state a point of view – not just to belong to a club. This is only a step away from the absence of psychotic competitiveness evident in the Classical world. We can, if we choose to accept diversity as valuable, elect to live in a world where freedom of choice extends to the eye and ear, as well as to the polling booth. We can restore to the objects we buy their essential purity, by a frank admission of their spiritual magic. We can, in short, acknowledge reverence – for literal things: wool and stone, plastic and steel, electricity and lasers, words and sounds – as an essential component of a full life. If we ignore the pundits whose credentials as arbiters of taste pale beside the rank, privilege or potency of the larger-than-life characters in this book, we can withdraw from the 'style wars' which feed contemporary journalists into a personal satisfaction which will enhance our own days, and thus the tone of our society. We can return to that ancient simplicity which did not mean austerity, that life-enhancing complexity of response defined by the Latin maxim, 'one does not dispute matters of taste'.

Bibliography

Abbati, Francesco (ed.), *Art Nouveau, The Style of the 1890s*, trans. E. Evans, London 1972

Barrow, Andrew, *Gossip: A History of High Society from 1920–1970*, London 1978

Battersby, Martin, *The World of Art Nouveau*, London 1968

Beaton, Cecil, *The Best of Beaton*, London 1968

Beaton, Cecil, Diaries: *The Wandering Years (1922–39)*, Boston 1961; *The Years Between (1939–44)*, New York 1965; *The Parting Years (1963–74)*, London 1978

Brown, Frederick, *An Impersonation of Angels: A Biography of Jean Cocteau*, New York 1968

Brunhammer, Yvonne, *The Nineteen-Twenties Style*, trans. Raymond Rudorff, London 1969

Buckle, Richard, *Nijinsky*, London 1971

Buckle, Richard, *Diaghilev*, London 1976

Burgess, Anthony, *A Clockwork Orange*, London and New York 1963

Chanel, Pierre (ed.), *Jean Cocteau, Poète Graphique*, Paris 1975

Charles-Roux, Edmonde, *Chanel and her World*, London 1981

Cocteau, Jean, *Professional Secrets*, trans. Richard Howard, New York 1972

Cooper, Nicholas, *The Opulent Eye: Late Victorian and Edwardian Taste in Interior Design*, London 1976

Core, Philip McCammon, *The Palm-Fronde Alphabet*, privately printed 1965

Dars, Célestine, *Images of Deception, The Art of Trompe L'Oeil*, Oxford 1979

Diesbach, Ghislain de, *Philippe Jullian 1919–1977*, Paris 1980

Donaldson, Frances, *Edward VIII*, London 1944

Dunlop, Ian, *The Shock of the New*, London 1972

Emboden, William, *Sarah Bernhardt*, London 1974

Erté, *Things I Remember, An Autobiography*, London 1975

Field, Andrew, *Djuna, The Life and Times of Djuna Barnes*, New York 1983

Flint, R. W. (ed.), *Marinetti: Selected Writings*, New York 1972

Fulop-Miller, René and Joseph Gregor, *The Russian Theatre, Its Character and History*, trans. Paul England, London 1930

Gérard, Max, *Dali ... Dali ... Dali*, New York 1974

Griffith, Richard and Arthur Mayer, *The Movies*, rev. edn. New York 1970

Guggenheim, Peggy, *Out of this Century, Confessions of an Art Addict*, London 1980

Hillier, Bevis, *Art Deco of the Twenties and Thirties*, London 1968

Hobhouse, Janet, *Everybody Who Was Anybody: A Biography of Gertrude Stein*, New York 1975

Hockney, David, *David Hockney*, London 1976

Howell, Georgina, *In Vogue: Six Decades of Fashion*, London 1975

Huysmans, J.-K., *Against Nature*, trans. Robert Baldick, London 1959

Jackson, Holbrook, *The Eighteen-Nineties, A Review of Art and Ideas*, New York 1923

Johnson, Carry, *The Story of Oi: A View from the Dead-end of The Street*, Manchester 1981

Jullian, Philippe, *Jean Lorrain ou le Satyricon 1900*, Paris 1974

Jullian, Philippe, *Les Styles*, Paris 1961

Jullian, Philippe, *Prince of Aesthetes: Count Robert de Montesquiou 1955–1921*, trans. J. Haylock and F. King, London 1967

Keenan, Brigid, *Dior in Vogue*, London 1981

King, Viva, *The Weeping and the Laughter*, London 1976

Kochno, Boris, *Diaghilev and the Ballets Russes*, trans. Adrienne Roulke, New York 1970

Kubrick, Stanley, *A Clockwork Orange*, based on the novel by Anthony Burgess, New York 1972

Latour, Anny, *Kings of Fashion*, trans. Mervyn Savill, London 1958

Label, Robert, *Marcel Duchamp*, trans. G. H. Hamilton, New York 1959

Lucie-Smith, Edward, *Symbolist Art*, London 1972

Lynam, Ruth (ed.), *Paris Fashions: The Great Designers and their Creations*, London 1972

McMullen, Roy, *Victorian Outsider, a Biography of J. A. M. Whistler*, London 1973

Melly, George, *Rum, Bum and Concertina*, London 1977

Moers, Ellen, *The Dandy: Brummel to Beerbohm*, New York 1960

Nicolson, Harold, *Diaries and Letters 1930–1939*, ed. Nigel Nicolson, London 1966

Noailles, Comtesse Mathieu de, *Les Eblouissements*, Paris n.d.

Ormond, Richard, *John Singer Sargent: Paintings, Drawings, Watercolours*, London and New York 1970

Percival, John, *The World of Diaghilev*, London 1971

Pop, Iggy, with Anne Wehrer, *I Need More, I Need More*, Princeton 1982

Rheims, Maurice, *The Flowering of Art Nouveau*, trans. Patrick Evans, New York n.d.

Skinner, Cornelia Otis, *Madame Sarah Bernhardt*, trans. P. Jullian, Paris 1968

Smith, Jane S., *Elsie de Wolfe, A Life in the High Style*, New York 1982

Snowdon, *Assignments*, London 1972

Snowdon, *Personal View*, London 1979

Spencer, Charles, *The World of Serge Diaghilev*, London 1974

Steegmuller, Francis, *Cocteau, A Biography*, Boston 1970

Stein, Jean, *Edie. An American Biography*, New York 1982

Vreeland, Diana, *Allure*, New York 1980

Waldberg, Patrick, *Surrealism*, London 1965

Warhol, Andy with Bob Colacello, *Andy Warhol's Exposures*, London 1979

Warhol, Andy, *A*, New York 1972

Warhol, Andy, *Andy Warhol's Index Book*, New York 1967

Whistler, Lawrence, *Rex Whistler 1905–1944. His Life and His Drawings*, London 1948

White, Palmer, *Poiret*, London 1973

Wilson, Sandy and Jon Rose, *Who's Who for Beginners*, London 1957

Wishart, Michael, *High Diver*, London 1977

Wolfe, Elsie de, *After All*, London 1935

Acknowledgements

Archivi Alinari, Florence: 96; 101; 103.
Aurum Press Limited, London: 29.
BBC Hulton Picture Library, London: 1; 22; 32; 67; 86; 89; 90; 97; 180.
Cecil Beaton, courtesy Eileen Hose, Salisbury: 117.
Cecil Beaton, courtesy Sotheby's London: 5; 53; 55; 58; 108; 109; 110; 114; 116; 122; 123; 137; 142.
Denise Bellon, Paris: 129; 133.
Bibliothèque Nationale, Paris: 11; 26.
The Bridgeman Art Library, London: 73 (A.D.A.G.P. 1984).
The Brooklyn Museum, New York: 27.
Camera Press Limited, London: 52; 107; 121; 168.
Leo Castelli Gallery, New York: 164.
CBS Records, London: 190.
Charisma Records Limited, London: 10; 196; 197.
Jean-Loup Charmet, Paris: 25.
Art Institute of Chicago: 14.
The Daily Telegraph Colour Library, London: 141.
Dallas Museum of Art, Foundation for the Arts Collection, gift of the artist: 80.
Jesse Davis, London: 119.
Christian Dior, Paris: 57.
Tony Duquette, Los Angeles: 49; 61; 62; 63; 65; 66.
Farabolafoto, Milan: 87; 92; 104.
The Frick Collection, New York: 21.
Globe Photos Inc, New York: 156; 161; 169.
The Granger Collection, New York: 3; 48.
Howard Grey, London: 43.
The Peggy Guggenheim Collection, Venice (The Solomon R. Guggenheim Foundation): 150 (Aschieri); 158; 160 (Mirko Lion).
Roger Guillemot/Edimedia, Paris: 28; 130; 135 (S.P.A.D.E.M 1984); 138; 143.
Roger Guillemot/Top/Rapho, Paris: 126.
Ronald Henbury, Ingatestone, Essex: 178.
Michael Holford, Loughton, Essex: 16.
The Houghton Library, Harvard University, Cambridge, Massachusetts: 17; 18
Imperial War Museum, London: 105.
Philip Johnson, New York: 82.
Keystone Press Agency Limited, London: 153; 162; 165; 166; 174.
The Kobal Collection, London: 127; 140; 171; 172; 173; 175; 177.
Mander & Mitchenson Theatre Collection, London: 30.
Felix Marcilhac, Paris: 60.

Neil Matthews, London: 194.
The Mayor Gallery, London: 136.
Malcolm McLaren, London: 189; 198.
Memphis Furniture, Milan: 191
The Metropolitan Museum of Art, New York (The Alfred Stieglitz Collection, 1949): 71.
Moro, Rome: 7; 95; 99; 106.
Musée des Arts Décoratifs, Paris: 131.
Musée National d'Art Moderne, Centre Georges Pompidou, Paris: 134.
Musées Nationaux, Paris: 23; 46.
The Museum of Modern Art, New York: 83; 88 (Lillie P. Bliss Bequest).
Galleria Narciso, Turin: 102 (Private Collection, Italy).
The National Film Archive, London – Paramount Pictures, New York: 44; MGM, California: 94; Columbia Warner, London: 124; 167; 179; 183; 184.
The National Trust, Llandudno: 111.
The National Trust Photographic Library, London: 112; 113.
Peter Newark's Western Americana, Bath: 85.
Ormond Family, England: 15.
Michael Parkin Fine Art Limited, London: 115.
Georges Platt-Lynes, collection Paul Cadmus, USA: 81.
Popperfoto, London: 6; 8; 13; 56; 93; 118; 144.
Practical Styling, London: 192; 193.
RCA Limited, London: 195.
Rex Features Limited, London: 170; 176.
Roger-Viollet, Paris: 2; 24; 33; 35; 36; 38; 39; 40; 41; 100; 128; 132; 139.
The Royal Photographic Society, Bath: 70.
Gabor J. F. Scott, London: 182; 188.
Archives of American Art, Smithsonian Institution, Washington D.C.: 19 (Collection of Artists Photos); 74 (Walt Kuhn Papers).
James Stevens Curl, Winchester: 98.
Laurent Sully Jaulmes/Galerie Alain Blondel, Paris: 91 (S.P.A.D.E.M. 1984)
Topham Picture Library, Edenbridge, Kent: 9; 59; 64; 155; 163; 185; 187.
United Press International, New York: 4; 50; 51; 54; 75; 78; 84.
Virgin Records Limited, London: 186.
Whitney Museum of American Art. Gift of the Friends of the Whitney Museum of American Art. Charles Simon (and purchase): 72.

Index